Reprints of Economic Classics

THE

PAMPHLETS

OF

THOMAS ROBERT MALTHUS

Also by THOMAS ROBERT MALTHUS

In REPRINTS OF ECONOMIC CLASSICS

THE

PAMPHLETS

OF

THOMAS ROBERT MALTHUS

REPRINTS OF ECONOMIC CLASSICS

AUGUSTUS M. KELLEY · PUBLISHERS
NEW YORK 1970

First Published In This Edition 1970

Reprinted 1970 By
Augustus M. Kelley · Publishers
REPRINTS OF ECONOMIC CLASSICS
New York New York 10001

· · · · · · · · · · · · · · · · · ·

I S B N 0-678-00646-6
L C N 77-117389

· · · · · · · · · · · · · · · · · ·

PRINTED IN THE UNITED STATES OF AMERICA
by SENTRY PRESS, NEW YORK, N. Y. 10019

TABLE OF CONTENTS

AN INVESTIGATION OF THE CAUSE
OF THE PRESENT HIGH PRICE
OF PROVISIONS

(THIRD EDITION, 1800)

AN

INVESTIGATION

OF

The Cause

OF THE PRESENT

HIGH PRICE OF PROVISIONS:

CONTAINING

AN ILLUSTRATION OF THE NATURE AND
LIMITS OF FAIR PRICE IN TIME OF
SCARCITY;

AND ITS

APPLICATION TO THE PARTICULAR CIRCUM-
STANCES OF THIS COUNTRY.

BY THE AUTHOR OF THE ESSAY ON THE
PRINCIPLE OF POPULATION.

THIRD EDITION.

LONDON:

PRINTED FOR

J. JOHNSON, IN ST. PAUL'S-CHURCH-YARD,

BY DAVIS, TAYLOR, AND WILKS, CHANCERY-LANE.

1800.

AN
INVESTIGATION,
&c.

———

AMONG the many causes that have been assigned of the present high price of provisions, I am much inclined to suspect, that the principal one has hitherto escaped detection; at least, in the discussions on the subject, either in print or conversation, which have fallen within my knowledge, the cause, which I conceive to have operated most strongly towards increasing the price of the necessaries of life, has not yet been suggested. There are some disorders, which, though they scarcely admit of a cure, or even of any considerable mitigation, are still capable of being made greatly worse. In such misfortunes it is of great importance to know the desperate nature of the disease. The next step to the alleviation of pain, is the bearing it with composure, and not aggravating it by impatience and irritation.||

It cannot admit of a doubt with persons of sense and information, that, during the last year, there was a scarcity, to a certain extent, of all sorts of grain; but it must be at the same time acknowledged, that the price was higher than the degree of that scarcity would at first sight appear to warrant.

In the Summer of 1799, in the course of a northern tour, I passed through Sweden. There was at that time a general dearth of corn throughout the country, owing to a long drought the preceding year. In the province of Wurmland, adjoining to Norway, it approached almost to a famine, and the lower classes of people suffered most severe distress. At the time we were passing through that part of the country, which was in July, they were reduced to two most miserable substitutes for bread; one, made of the inner bark of the fir, and the other, of the common sorrel dried, and powdered. These substances, though made into the usual shape of their rye bread, had no affinity to it whatever in taste, and but very little, I believe, in nourishment, as the effects of this miserable food were but too visible in their pallid and unhealthy countenances.

There could be little doubt, that the degree of scarcity then prevailing in that part of Sweden, was considerably greater than any we have hitherto||experienced here; and yet, as far as we could learn; the price of rye, which is the grain principally used for bread, had not risen above double its usual average; whereas in this country last year, in a scarcity, that must be acknowledged to be very greatly inferior in degree, wheat rose to above three times its former price.

The continuation of extraordinary high prices, after a harvest that was at one time looked forward to as abundant, has contributed still more to astonish and perplex the public mind. Many men of sense have joined in the universal cry of the common people, that there must be roguery somewhere; and the general indignation has fallen upon monopolizers, forestallers, and regraters—words, that are vented from every mouth with fearful execrations, and are applied indiscriminately to all middle men whatever, to every kind of trader that goes between the grower of the commodity and the consumer.

This popular clamour, headed by the Lord Chief Justice, and enforced throughout the country by the instructions of the grand juries, must make every reflecting mind tremble for the future supply of our markets. I cannot but think, therefore, that I should do an acceptable service, if I could succeed in accounting for the present||high price of the necessaries of life, without criminating a class of men, who, I believe, have been accused unjustly, and who, every political economist must know, are absolutely necessary in the complicated machinery that distributes the provisions and other commodities of a large nation.

I ought first to premise, however, that I am not interested in this question, further than as a lover of truth, and a well-wisher to my country. I have no sort of connection whatever with any of these middle men or great farmers, who are now the objects of public indigation: and, as an individual with a small fixed income, I am certainly among that class of persons on whom the high price of provisions must fall the heaviest.

To proceed to the point: I am most strongly inclined to suspect, that the attempt in most parts of the kingdom to increase the parish allowances in proportion to the price of corn, combined with the riches of the country, which have enabled it to proceed as far as it has done in this attempt, is, comparatively speaking, the sole cause[1], which has occasioned the price of provisions in this country to rise so much higher than the degree||of scarcity would seem to warrant, so much higher than it would do in any other country where this cause did not operate.

It may appear, perhaps, at first, to the reader, that this cause is inadequate to the effect we experience; but, if he will kindly allow me a few minutes of patient and candid attention, I hope I shall be able to convince him, that it is not only adequate to produce the present high price of provisions of which we complain; but, admitting a real scarcity, that the attempt to carry it generally into execution, might raise the quartern loaf before the expiration of a year, to as many shillings as it is now pence.

Adam Smith has most justly stated, that the actual price at which a commodity is sold, is compounded of its natural price, the price at which it can be brought to market, allowing the usual profit in times of moderate plenty, and the proportion of the supply to the demand. When any commodity is scarce, its natural price is necessarily forgotten, and its actual price is regulated by the excess of the demand above the supply.

Let us suppose a commodity in great request by fifty people, but of which, from some failure in its

---

[1] It will be observed that I am not now speaking of the causes that may have contributed to the actual scarcity; but of the cause of the very high price of provisions in proportion to the actual *degree* of that scarcity.

production, there is only sufficient to supply forty. If the fortieth man from the top have two||shillings which he can spend in this commodity, and the thirty-nine above him, more, in various proportions, and the ten below, all less, the actual price of the article, according to the genuine principles of trade, will be two shillings. If more be asked, the whole will not be sold, because there are only forty who have as much as two shillings to spend in the article; and there is no reason for asking less, because the whole may be disposed of at that sum.

Let us suppose, now, that somebody gives the ten poor men, who were excluded, a shilling apiece. The whole fifty can now offer two shillings, the price which was before asked. According to every genuine principle of fair trading, the commodity must immediately rise. If it do not, I would ask, upon what principle are ten, out of the fifty who are all able to offer two shillings, to be rejected? For still, according to the supposition, there is only enough for forty. The two shillings of a poor man are just as good as the two shillings of a rich one; and, if we interfere to prevent the commodity from rising out of the reach of the poorest ten, whoever they may be, we must toss up, draw lots, raffle; or fight, to determine who are to be excluded. It would be beyond my present purpose, to enter into the question whe-||ther any of these modes would be more eligible, for the distribution of the commodities of a country, than the sordid distinction of money; but certainly, according to the customs of all civilized and enlightened nations, and according to every acknowledged principle of commercial dealing, the price must be allowed to rise to that point which will put it beyond the power of ten out of the fifty to purchase. This point will, perhaps, be half-a-crown or more, which will now become the price of the commodity. Let another shilling a-piece be given to the excluded ten: all will now be able to offer half-a-crown. The price must in consequence immediately rise to three shillings or more, and so on *toties quoties*.

In the progress of this operation the ten excluded would not be always entirely the same. The richest of the ten first excluded, would probably be raised above the poorest of the first forty. Small changes of this kind must take place. The additional allowances to the poorest, and the weight of the high prices on those above them, would tend to level the two orders; but, till a complete level had taken place, ten must be always excluded, and the price would always be fixed, as nearly as possible, at that sum which the fortieth man from the top could afford to give. This,||if the donatives were continued, would raise the commodity to an extraordinary price, without the supposition of any combination and conspiracy among the venders, or any kind of unfair dealing whatever.

The rise in the price of corn, and of other provisions, in this country, has been effected exactly in the same manner, though the operation may be a little more complicated; and I am firmly convinced, that it never could have reached its present height, but from the system of poor laws and parish allowances, which have operated precisely in the same mode as the donatives of a shilling in the instance I have just adduced.

The harvest of 1799 was bad, both in quality and quantity. Few people could deny that there appeared to be a very considerable deficiency of produce; and the price of the load of wheat rose in consequence almost immediately to £.20. I returned from the North in the beginning of November, and found the alarm so great and general, and the price of corn so high, that I remember thinking that it was probably fully adequate to the degree of the deficiency, and, taking into consideration the prospect of importation from the very early alarm, that it would not rise much higher during the year. In this conjecture, it‖appears that I was much mistaken; but I have very little doubt that in any other country equally rich, yet without the system of poor laws and parish allowances, the price would never have exceeded £.25 the load of wheat; and that this sum would have been sufficiently high to have excluded such a number of people from their usual consumption, as to make the deficient crop, with the quantity imported, last throughout the year.

The system of poor laws, and parish allowances, in this country, and I will add, to their honour, the humanity and generosity of the higher and middle classes of society, naturally and necessarily altered this state of things. The poor complained to the justices that their wages would not enable them to supply their families in the single article of bread. The justices very humanely, and I am far from saying improperly, listened to their complaints, inquired what was the smallest sum on which they could support their families, at the then price of wheat, and gave an order of relief on the parish accordingly. The poor were now enabled, for a short time, to purchase nearly their usual quantity of flour; but the stock in the country was not sufficient, even with the prospect of importation, to allow of the usual distribution||to all its members. The crop was consuming too fast. Every market day the demand exceeded the supply; and those whose business it was to judge on these subjects, felt convinced, that in a month or two the scarcity would be greater than it was at that time. Those who were able, therefore, kept back their corn. In so doing, they undoubtedly consulted their own interest; but they, as undoubtedly, whether with the intention or not is of no consequence, consulted the true interest of the state: for, if they had not kept it back, too much would have been consumed, and there would have been a famine instead of a scarcity at the end of the year.

The corn, therefore, naturally rose. The poor were again distressed. Fresh complaints were made to the justices, and a further relief granted; but, like the water from the mouth of Tantalus, the corn still slipped from the grasp of the poor; and rose again so as to disable them from purchasing a sufficiency to keep their families in health. The alarm now became still greater, and more general[2]. The justices in their individual capa-||cities were not thought competent to determine on the proper modes of relief in the present crisis, a general meeting of the magistrates was

---

[2] I am describing what took place in the neighbourhood where I then lived; and I have reason to believe that something nearly similar took place in most counties of the kingdom.

called, aided by the united wisdom of other gentlemen of the county; but the result was merely the
continuation and extension of the former system of
relief; and, to say the truth, I hardly see what else
could have been done. In some parishes this relief was
given in the shape of flour; in others, which was certainly better, in money, accompanied with a recom-
mendation not to spend the whole of it in wheaten
bread, but to adopt some other kind of food. All, however, went upon the principle of inquiring what was
the usual consumption of flour in the different families, and of enabling them to purchase nearly the
same quantity that they did before the scarcity. With
this additional command of money in the lower classes,
and the consequent increased consumption, the number of purchasers at the then price would naturally
exceed the supply. The corn would in consequence
continue rising. The poor's rates in many parishes
increased from four shillings in the pound to twelve;
the price of wheat necessarily kept pace with them;
and before the end of the year was at nearly forty
pounds a load; when pro-||bably without the opera-
tion of this cause it would not have exceeded twenty
or twenty-five.

Some of the poor would naturally make use of their
additional command of money to purchase butter,
cheese, bacon, pickled pork, rice, potatoes, &c. These
commodities are all more limited in quantity than
corn; and would, therefore, more suddenly feel the
increased demand. If butter, cheese, bacon, pickled
pork, and the coarser parts of meat, had continued at
their usual price, they would have been purchased by

so many, to come in aid of an inferior kind of bread, or to give a relish and additional nourishment to their potatoes and rice, that the supply would not have been half adequate to the quantity of these articles that was wanted. These commodities, therefore, rose as naturally and as necessarily as the corn; and, according to the genuine principles of fair trade, their price was fixed at that sum which only such a number could afford to give, as would enable the supply to answer the demand.

To fix upon this sum is the great object of every dealer and speculator in every commodity whatever, and about which he must, of course, exercise his private judgment. A reflecting||mind, far from being astonished that there are now and then errors in speculation, must feel much greater astonishment that there are so few; and that the supplies of a large nation, whether plentiful or scanty, should be distributed so equally throughout the year. Most happily for society, individual interest is, in these cases, so closely and intimately interwoven with the public interest, that one cannot gain or lose without a gain or loss to the other. The man who refuses to send his corn to market when it is at twenty pounds a load, because he thinks that in two months time it will be at thirty, if he be right in his judgment, and succeed in his speculation, is a positive and decided benefactor to the state; because he keeps his supply to that period when the state is much more in want of it; and if he and some others did not keep it back in that manner, instead of its being thirty in two months, it would be forty or fifty.

If he be wrong in his speculation, he loses perhaps very considerably himself, and the state suffers a little; because, had he brought his corn to market at twenty, the price would have fallen sooner, and the event shewed that there was corn enough in the country to allow of it; but the slight evil that the state suffers in this case||is almost wholly compensated by the glut in the market, when the corn is brought out, which makes the price fall below what it would have been otherwise.

I am far from saying that there can be no such thing as monopoly, and the other hard words that have been so much talked of. In a commodity of a confined nature, within the purchase of two or three large capitals, or of a company of merchants, we all know that it has often existed; and, in a very few instances, the article may have been in part destroyed, to enhance the price, as the Dutch Company destroyed the nutmeg trees in their spice islands: but in an article which is in so many hands as corn is, in this country, monopoly, to any pernicious extent, may safely be pronounced impossible. Where are the capitals, or where is the company of merchants, rich enough to buy such a quantity of corn, as would make it answer to them to destroy, or, which is the same thing, not to sell a great part of it? As they could not, by the greatest exertions, purchase one fourth of all the corn in the country, it is evident that, if any considerable part of their stock remained unsold, they would have enriched all the other dealers in corn at their own expense;||and would not have gained half so much in proportion to their capital as the rest of the farmers and cornfactors. If on the contrary all their stock sold, it would be a proof that the speculation had been just, and that the country had really benefited by it.

It seems now to be universally agreed, that the stock of old corn remaining on hand at the beginning of the harvest this year was unusually small, notwithstanding that the harvest came on nearly a month sooner than could have been expected in the beginning of June. This is a clear, decided, and unanswerable proof that there had been no speculations in corn that were prejudicial to the country. All that the large farmers and cornfactors had done, was to raise the corn to that price which excluded a sufficient number from their usual consumption, to enable the supply to last throughout the year. This price, however, has been most essentially and powerfully affected by the ability that has been given to the labouring poor, by means of parish allowances, of continuing to purchase wheat notwithstanding its extraordinary rise: and this ability must necessarily prevent the price of corn from falling very materially, till there is an actual glut in the market; for, while the whole stock will go off at||thirty pounds a load, it cannot, on any regular principle of trade, sink lower. I was in very great hopes, just before the harvest, that such a glut was about to take place; but it is now to be feared, from the nature of the present crop, that no such happy event can be hoped for during the year.

I do not know whether I have convinced my reader that the cause which I have assigned of the present extraordinary price of provisions is adequate to the effect; but I certainly feel most strongly convinced of it myself; and I cannot but believe that, if he differ from me, it can only be in degree, and from thinking that the principle of parish allowances has not yet been carried far enough to produce any material effect. With regard to the principle itself, if it were generally carried into execution, it appears to me capable almost of mathematical demonstration, that, granting a real scarcity of one-fourth, which could not be remedied by importation, it is adequate to the effecting any height of price that the proportion of the circulating medium to the quantity of corn daily consumed would admit.

It has often been proposed, and more than once I believe, in the House of Commons, to proportion the price of labour exactly to the||price of provisions. This, though it would be always a bad plan, might pass tolerably in years of moderate plenty, or in a country that was in the habit of a considerable exportation of grain. But let us see what would be its operation in a real scarcity. We suppose, for the sake of the argument, that by law every kind of labour is to be paid accurately in proportion to the price of corn, and that the rich are to be assessed to the utmost to support those in the same manner who are thrown out of employment, and fall upon the parish. We allow the scarcity to be an irremediable deficiency of one-fourth of all the provisions of the country. It is evident that, notwithstanding this deficiency, there would be no reason for economy in the labouring classes. The rise of their wages, or the parish allowances that they would receive, would enable them to purchase exactly the same quantity of corn, or other provisions, that they did before, whatever their price might be. The same quantity would of course be consumed; and, according to the regular principles of trade, as the stock continued diminishing, the price of all the necessaries of life would continue rising, in the most rapid and unexampled manner. The middle classes of society would very soon be blended||with the poor; and the largest fortunes could not long stand against the accumulated pressure of the extraordinary price of provisions, on the one hand, and the still more extraordinary assessments for allowances to those who had no other means of support, on the other. The cornfactors and farmers would undoubtedly be the last that suffered, but, at the expiration of the three quarters of a year, what they received with one hand, they must give away with the other; and a most complete levelling of all property would take place. All would have the same quantity of money. All the provisions of the country would be consumed; and all the people would starve together.

There is no kind of fear, that any such tragical event should ever happen in any country; but I allowed myself to make the supposition; because, it appears to me, that, in the complicated machinery of human society, the effect of any particular principle frequently escapes from the view, even of an attentive observer, if it be not magnified by pushing it to extremity.

I do not, however, by any means, intend to infer, from what I have said, that the parish allowances have been prejudicial to the state; or that, as far as the system has been hitherto||pursued, or is likely to be pursued, in this country, that it is not one of the best modes of relief that the circumstances of the case will admit. The system of the poor laws, in general, I certainly do most heartily condemn, as I have expressed in another place, but I am inclined to think that their operation in the present scarcity has been advantageous to the country. The principal benefit which they have produced, is exactly that which is most bitterly complained of—the high price of all the necessaries of life. The poor cry out loudly at this price; but, in so doing, they are very little aware of what they are about; for it has undoubtedly been owing to this price that a much greater number of them has not been starved.

It was calculated that there were only two-thirds of an average crop last year. Probably, even with the aid of all that we imported, the deficiency still remained a fifth or sixth. Supposing ten millions of people in the island; the whole of this deficiency, had things been left to their natural course, would have fallen almost exclusively on two, or perhaps three millions of the poorest inhabitants, a very considerable number of whom must in consequence have starved. The operation of the parish al-||lowances, by raising the price of provisions so high, caused the distress to be divided among five or six millions, perhaps, instead of two or three, and to be by no means unfelt even by the remainder of the population.

The high price, therefore, which is so much complained of by the poor, has essentially mitigated their distress by bringing down to their level two or three millions more, and making them almost equal sharers in the pressure of the scarcity.

The further effects of the high price have been to enforce a strict economy in all ranks of life; to encourage an extraordinary importation, and to animate the farmer by the powerful motive of self-interest to make every exertion to obtain as great a crop as possible the next year.

If economy, importation, and every possible encouragement to future production, have not the fairest chance of putting an end to the scarcity, I confess myself at a loss to say what better means can be substituted. I may undoubtedly on this subject be much mistaken; but to me, I own, they appear more calculated to answer the purpose intended, than the hanging any number of farmers and cornfactors that could be named.||

No inference, therefore, is meant to be drawn against what has been done for the relief of the poor in the present scarcity, though it has without doubt greatly raised the price of provisions. All that I contend for is, that we should be aware of the effect of what we ourselves have done, and not lay the blame on the wrong persons.

If the cause, which I have detailed, be sufficient to account for the present high price of provisions, without the supposition of any unfair dealing among the farmers and cornfactors, we ought surely to bear the present pressure like men labouring under a disorder that must have its course, and not throw obstacles in the way of returning plenty, and endanger the future supplies of our markets, by encouraging the popular clamour, and keeping the farmers and corn-dealers in perpetual fear for their lives and property.

To suppose that a year of scarcity can pass without distressing severely a large part of the inhabitants of a country, is to suppose a contradiction in the nature of things. I know of no other definition of a scarcity than the failure of the usual quantity of provisions; and if a great part of the people had but just enough before, they must undoubtedly have less than enough at||such a period. With regard to the scarcity being artificial, it appears to me so impossible, that, till it has been proved that some man or set of men, with a capital of twenty or thirty millions sterling, has bought up half the corn in the country, I own I must still disbelieve it. On this subject, however, I know that I differ from some very respectable friends of mine, among the common people, who say that it is quite impossible that there can be a real scarcity, because you may get what quantity of corn you please, if you have but money enough; and to say the truth, many persons, who ought to be better informed, argue exactly in the same way. I have often talked with labouring men on this subject, and endeavoured to show them, that if they, or I, had a great deal of money, and other people had but little, we could undoubtedly buy what quantity of corn we liked, by taking away the shares of those who were less rich; but that if all the people had the same sum, and that there was not enough corn in the country to supply all, we could not get what we wanted for money, though we possessed millions. I never found, however, that my rhetoric produced much impression.

The cry at present is in favour of small farms,|| and against middle men. No two clamours can well be more inconsistent with each other, as the destruction of the middle men would, I conceive, necessarily involve with it the destruction of small farmers. The small farmer requires a quick return of his scanty capital to enable him to pay his rent and his workmen; and must therefore send his corn to market almost immediately after harvest. If he were required to perform the office of corn-dealer, as well as farmer, and wait to regulate his supplies to the demands of the markets, a double capital would be absolutely necessary to him, and not having that, he would be ruined.

Many men of sense and information have attributed the dearness of provisions to the quantity of paper in circulation. There was undoubtedly great reason for apprehension, that when, by the stoppage of the Bank to pay in specie, the emission of paper ceased to have its natural check, the circulation would be overloaded with this currency; but this certainly could not have taken place to any considerable extent without a sensible depreciation of bank notes in comparison with specie. As this depreciation did not happen, the progress of the evil must have been slow and gradual, and never||could have produced the sudden and extraordinary rise in the price of provisions which was so sensibly felt last year, after a season of moderate cheapness, subsequent to the stoppage of the Bank.

There is one circumstance, however, that ought to be attended to. To circulate the same, or nearly the same[3], quantity of commodities through a country, when they bear a much higher price, must require a greater quantity of the medium, whatever that may be. The circulation naturally takes up more. It is probable, therefore, that the Bank has found it necessary to issue a greater number of its notes on this account. Or, if it has not, this deficiency has been supplied by the country bankers, who have found that their notes now stay out longer, and in greater quantity, than they did before the scarcity, which may tempt many to overtrade their capitals. If the quantity of paper, therefore, in circulation has greatly increased during the last year, I should be inclined to consider it rather as the effect than the cause of the high price of provisions. This fulness of circulating||medium, however, will be one of the obstacles in the way to returning cheapness.

The public attention is now fixed with anxiety towards the meeting of Parliament, which is to relieve us from our present difficulties; but the more considerate do not feel very sanguine on this subject, knowing how little is to be done in this species of distress by legislative interference. We interfere to fix the assize of bread. Perhaps one of the best interferences of the Legislature, in the present instance, would be to abolish that assize. I have certainly no tendency to believe in combinations and conspiracies; but the great interval that elapses between the fall of wheat and the fall of flour, compared with the quick succession of the rise of flour to the rise of wheat, would

---

[3] In a scarcity the quantity of commodities in circulation is probably not so great as in years of plenty.

almost tempt one to suppose, that there might be some little management in the return of the meal weighers to the Lord Mayor. If the public suffer in this instance, it is evidently owing to the assize, without which, the opportunity of any such management would not exist. And what occasion can there be for an assize in a city like London, in which there are so many bakers? If such a regulation were ever necessary, it would appear to be most so in a country village or small town,||where perhaps there is but one person in the trade, and who might, therefore, for a time, have an opportunity of imposing on his customers; but this could not take place where there was such room for competition as in London. If there were no assize, more attention would be constantly paid to the weight and quality of the bread bought; and the bakers who sold the best in these two respects would have the most custom. The removal of this regulation would remove, in a great measure, the difficulty about brown bread, and a much greater quantity of it would probably be consumed.

The soup-shops, and every attempt to make a nourishing and palatable food of what was before not in use among the common people, must evidently be of great service in the present distress.

It is a fact now generally acknowledged, and it has lately received an official sanction in a letter of the Duke of Portland to the Lord Lieutenant of the county of Oxford, that of late years, even in the best seasons, we have not grown corn sufficient for our own consumption; whereas, twenty years ago, we were in the constant habit of exporting grain to a very considerable amount. Though we may suppose that||the agriculture of the country has not been increasing, as it ought to have done, during this period; yet we cannot well imagine that it has gone backwards. To what then can we attribute the present inability in the country to support its inhabitants, but to the increase of population? I own that I cannot but consider the late severe pressures of distress on every deficiency in our crops, as a very strong exemplification of a principle which I endeavoured to explain in an essay published about two years ago, entitled, *An Essay on the Principle of Population, as it affects the future Improvement of Society.* It was considered by many who read it, merely as a specious argument, inapplicable to the present state of society; because it contradicted some preconceived opinions on these subjects. Two years reflection have, however, served strongly to convince me of the truth of the principle there advanced, and of its being the real cause of the continued depression and poverty of the lower classes of society, of the total inadequacy of all the present establishments in their favour to relieve them, and of the periodical returns of such seasons of distress as we have of late experienced.||

The essay has now been out of print above a year; but I have deferred giving another edition of it in the hope of being able to make it more worthy of the public attention, by applying the principle directly and exclusively to the existing state of society, and endeavouring to illustrate the power and universality of its operation from the best authenticated accounts that we have of the state of other countries. Particular engagements in the former part of the time, and some most unforseen and unfortunate interruptions latterly, have hitherto prevented me from turning my attention, with any effect, towards this subject. I still, however, have it in view. In the mean time I hope that this hasty attempt to add my mite to the public stock of information, in the present emergency, will be received with candour.

THE END.

A LETTER TO
SAMUEL WHITBREAD, ESQ., M.P.,
ON HIS PROPOSED BILL FOR THE
AMENDMENT OF THE POOR LAWS

(SECOND EDITION, 1807)

A

LETTER

TO

SAMUEL WHITBREAD, ESQ. M.P.

ON HIS

PROPOSED BILL

FOR

THE AMENDMENT

OF THE

POOR LAWS.

BY THE

REV. T. R. MALTHUS, A.M.

LATE FELLOW OF JESUS COLLEGE,

CAMBRIDGE;

AND AUTHOR OF THE ESSAY ON THE PRINCIPLE OF POPULATION.

THE SECOND EDITION.

LONDON:

PRINTED FOR J. JOHNSON, ST. PAUL'S CHURCHYARD,

AND J. HATCHARD, PICCADILLY,

By Wood and Innes, Poppin's Court, Fleet-Street.

1807.

A
LETTER,
&c.

SIR;

As you have done me the honour to refer more than
once to my work on Population, and to express your
conviction of the truth of its fundamental principles,
I trust you will pardon the liberty I take in offering
to you a few remarks, which an attentive perusal of
your bill on the Poor Laws has suggested. The acknowledged candour and uprightness of your character and the distinguished talents which you have on
all occasions shown, whenever the service of your
Country has called them into action, are pledges to
me, that you are anxious to collect informa-||tion
from every quarter where it can be attained; and
though you are little likely to be unduly biassed
either by authorities or numbers, yet that you stand
on too high ground to be afraid of retracting or modi-
fying any proposition which you may afterwards see
reason to think would not be attended with the effects
which it appeared at first to promise.

The experience of the last two hundred years, and
the circumstances which have called for the present

31

bill, are convincing proofs, that in the establishment of a satisfactory provision for the poor, the efforts of the ablest legislators have been repeatedly foiled. That the cause of these reiterated failures is to be found in those principles which I have endeavoured to explain in the Work to which you have referred, is a truth of which I feel the fullest confidence; but I am very far indeed from the presumption of supposing that the plan which I there suggested,||or any other that I could offer, would approach towards an adequate remedy for the evils which it has been the constant object of the legislature to remove. Indeed, from the developement of those principles it would appear that such a remedy is not to be expected.

It was denounced from divine authority to the inhabitants of the land of Canaan "that the poor should never cease from among them[1];" and the history of every country with which we are acquainted abundantly proves that the denunciation never has been, or will be, confined to a single nation. It was in fact a declaration of one of those difficulties with which it is the lot of humanity constantly to contend, and which as they can never be completely overcome without perfect virtue, seem to be destined to furnish un-||ceasing motives to the exercise and improvement both of our intellectual energies and our moral feelings.

But though to banish poverty from society be a task which, if not absolutely impossible, is clearly beyond the power of legislative regulations; yet the slightest glance at the state of different countries will indicate such important variations in the pressure of

---

[1] Deut. xv., 2.

this evil, as to give us the best grounded hopes of being able to lighten a burden which we cannot remove. In this noble and animating task however we must expect to meet with difficulties of no inconsiderable magnitude on every side to which we turn our view. And this consideration makes it pre-eminently the duty of the legislature, while it violates no positive precepts of morality, to be guided in its decisions by general rather than particular consequences.||

The compulsory provision for the poor in this country has, you will allow, produced effects which follow almost necessarily from the principle of population. The mere pecuniary consideration of the rapid increase of the rates of late years, though a point on which much stress has been laid, is not that which I consider as of the greatest importance; but the cause of this rapid increase, the increasing proportion of the dependent poor, appears to me to be a subject so truly alarming, as in some degree to threaten the extinction of all honourable feeling and spirit among the lower ranks of society, and to degrade and depress the condition of a very large and most important part of the community.

Under this impression I ventured to propose a plan for the gradual abolition of a system, which it was acknowledged had produced effects very different from those which had||been expected. And I still think that if we weigh on the one hand the great quantity of subjection and dependence which the poor laws create, together with the kind of relief which they afford, against the greater degree of freedom and the higher wages which would be the necessary consequence of their abolition, it will be difficult to believe that the mass of comfort and happiness would not be greater on the latter supposition, although the few that were then in distress would have no other resource than voluntary charity.

But though I think that the difficulties attending this state of things would be more than compensated by its advantages; yet after a compulsory provision for the poor had been so long established in this country, I am aware that these difficulties would be so strongly felt, and indeed I feel them so strongly myself, that I should be very sorry to||see any legislative regulation founded on the plan I have proposed, till the higher and middle classes of society were generally convinced of its necessity, and till the poor themselves could be made to understand that they had purchased their right to a provision by law, by too great and extensive a sacrifice of their liberty and happiness.

I cannot however think that it is either just or wise to dwell particularly on these difficulties, or to characterise as harsh and severe any propositions which may leave them to be provided for by voluntary charity—by those feelings which Providence seems to have implanted in our breasts for that express purpose, and which cannot but be materially impaired by the substitution of positive laws. It should be recollected that a compulsory provision for the poor is almost peculiar to England, and that there are many parts of the Continent without such a|| provision, and without those pre-eminent advantages of government which Englishmen enjoy, where the condition of the lower classes is superior. That cases of individual distress must occur in these countries, no person can for a moment doubt; but as there is no habitual dependence on a legal provision, the number is comparatively small; and I have never heard of any of those consequences of the absence of Poor Laws, which have sometimes been contemplated by warm imaginations, in the case of their abolition here.

The subject is besides peculiarly complex and delicate. To you who have made it your study, I can confidently appeal for the justice of my application of Mr. Hume's remark on the science of politics[2], to every plan for im-||proving the condition of the lower classes of society. First appearances indeed are in this branch of the science still more deceitful than in any other; and the partial and immediate effects of a particular mode of giving relief are often directly opposite to the general and permanent consequences. This circumstance renders all inquires of the kind remarkably open to misconstruction; and those who have not had leisure to pay that attention to the subject which its peculiar intricacy demands, if they hear one or two detached passages noticed by their friends which contradict their first feelings and apprehensions, are naturally disposed to be prejudiced against the whole Work in which they are found. If for a moment during your late Speech you gave the sanction of your authority to these prejudices, I am con-

---

[2] "Of all sciences, there is none where first appearances are more deceitful than in politics." Hume, Essay xi. vol. 1, p. 416.— He is led to this remark when speaking of Foundling Hospitals, which evidently belong to that branch of the science which is at present under discussion.

vinced that it was not really your intention to increase them; but that, in legislating on a point in which the interests of so large a part of the community are concerned, it is your great||wish that the legislature should not be prevented by partial and temporary considerations from steadily pursuing that system, which promises best to promote and secure the permanent happiness of the lower classes of society. There are not many laws either human or divine, which in particular instances do not appear harsh and unequal; but if on that account we were to be deprived of the guide of general rules, we should lose at once the best security of order, virtue, and happiness among men.

To those who know me personally, I feel that I have no occasion to defend my character from the imputation of hardness of heart; and to those who do not, I can only express my confidence that when they have attended to the subject as much as I have, they will be convinced that I have not admitted a single proposition which appears to detract from the present comforts and gratifications of the poor, without very strong||grounds for believing that it would be more than compensated to them by the general and permanent improvement of their condition.

The moral obligation of private, active, and discriminate charity I have endeavoured to enforce in the strongest language of which I was capable; and if I have denied the *natural right* of the poor to support, it is solely, to use the language of Sir F. M. Eden, after his able and laborious Enquiry into the State of the Poor, because "it may be doubted whether any right, the gratification of which seems to be impracticable, can be said to exist." To those who do not admit this conclusion, the denial of such a right may appear to be unfavourable to the poor. But those who are convinced of its truth, may, with the most anxious desire of extending the comforts and elevating the condition of the lower classes of society, rationally express their apprehensions, that the attempt to sanction by law|| a right which in the nature of things cannot be adequately gratified, may terminate in disappointment, irritation, and aggravated poverty.

With regard to the large sum which is collected from the higher classes of society for the support of the poor, I can safely say, that in the discussion of the question it has always been with me a most subordinate consideration.

I should indeed think that the whole, or a much greater sum, was well applied, if it merely relieved the comparatively few that would be in want, if there were no public provision for them, without the fatal and unavoidable consequence of continually increasing their number, and depressing the condition of those who were struggling to maintain themselves in independence. Were it possible to fix the number of the poor and to avoid the further depression of the independent labourer, I should be the first to||propose that those who were actually in want should be most liberally relieved, and that they should receive it as a right, and not as a bounty.

I ought to apologize for detaining you so long from the immediate subject of this letter; but I am sure your own feelings will tell you, that though I must be prepared to hear unmoved all those accusations of "hardness of heart" which appear to me to be the result of ignorance or malice, yet that any remark of the same kind coming from an enlightened and distinguished member of the British Senate cannot but give me pain, although accompanied by expressions of respect for my understanding.

But to proceed to the point. Putting all idea of the abolition of the Poor Laws out of the question, let us consider the general principles on which they ought to be improved. And here we are quite agreed, that the great object||should be, to elevate as much as possible the general character of the lower classes of the community, and to draw a more marked line between the dependent and independent labourer.

The plan of general education, which you have proposed, is admirably calculated to attain the first object; and should you only be able to accomplish this part of your Bill, you will in my opinion confer a most important benefit on your Country. The regulations which you have suggested in the mode of supporting those who are dependent on the parish, and the distinctions that you would introduce between the idle and the industrious, though not entirely free from objection[3], seem on the whole calculated to ac-

---

[3] I doubt the practicability of making the criminal poor wear marks; though it is certainly true that a man who has brought himself and family on the parish by his own idleness and vices, deserves to be thus distinguished from those who have been only unfortunate. With regard to the honorary badges proposed, though they might produce some good effects when distributed by a particular nobleman of high character; yet as a general measure I think they would be inefficient, particularly on account of the chance of their being improperly bestowed.

complish||the end which they have in view. But there are other regulations, to the effects of which I look forward with considerable doubt and apprehension.

The principal object of these apprehensions is the operation of the clause which empowers parishes to build cottages, combined with that which determines every kind of property to be rateable. Though these two clauses are unquestionably calculated to produce present comfort and relief; yet I much fear that their ultimate effects may be of a very different nature, and may tend powerfully to counteract the general principles on which your whole system of improvement is founded.||

The operations of the Poor Laws are so complicated, that it is almost impossible to take in at one view all their different bearings and relations. The establishment of them, one should naturally expect, would produce in any country a larger proportion of births and marriages than was usual *cæteris paribus* in others. But in England it appears that the proportion of births and marriages to the whole population is less than in most of the other countries of Europe; and though this circumstance is principally to be accounted for from other causes, yet it affords decisive evidence that the poor laws do not encourage early marriages *so much* as might naturally be expected.

The specific cause of this unexpected effect is, I have little doubt, the difficulty of procuring habitations. As the great burden of the poor's rates falls upon the land, it is natural that landlords should be fearful of building cottages except||where the demand for labour is absolutely urgent; and they will often submit, or at least oblige their tenants to submit, to an occasional scarcity of hands, rather than run the risk of fixing on their estates a permanent increase of rates. Under this difficulty of procuring habitations, which I have reason to think is very considerable, and which indeed I stated in the last edition of my work as the principal reason why the Poor Laws had not been so extensive and prejudicial in their effects as might have been expected, the rates have not only increased during late years with unusual rapidity; but (what is the only just criterion) the number of the dependent poor continually bears a greater proportion to the whole population. And it is highly probable that if this difficulty be removed by any of the regulations in your Bill, we shall soon see the proportion increased in a much greater degree than has ever hitherto been experienced.||

Such is the tendency to form early connections, that with the encouragement of a sufficient number of tenements, I have very little doubt that the population might be so pushed, and such a quantity of labour in time thrown into the market, as to render the condition of the independent labourer absolutely hopeless, and to make the common wages of day labour insufficient to support a single child without parish assistance.

I am very far from meaning to say that your Bill, as at present constituted, will certainly produce this effect; but I wish you to consider particularly how far it may have this tendency. You will probably alledge that under your Bill both the landlords and the parishes will still have a strong interest not to build fresh tenements unless called for by the increasing demand for labour. But it appears to me that your proposal||for making every kind of productive capital rateable[4], will effect a most important alteration in this interest.

If the burden of the poor's rates were really divided equally among all sorts of property, I am afraid it might be shown, from incontrovertible principles of political economy, that it would be a pecuniary advantage to all those who employ labour, and who would according to your Bill have the principal influence in all the determinations of Vestries, to push this encouragement to population to a considerable extent; because, in the employment of their capital, they would gain much more by the cheapness of labour, than they would lose by the payment of their rates.||

Of this, I think, you will be convinced, if you consider, in the first place, that when the rate of the increase of population depends exclusively on the wages of labour, the unmarried must be paid as high as the married; but that in the application of the poor laws to the encouragement of population, the assistance is only given to those who have families. Upon the latter system therefore a greater supply of labour may be obtained by an equal cost, and an equal supply at a less cost. In the next place, the capitalist would not only on this account employ his money more eco-

---

[4] I should think that very considerable difficulties would occur in rating personal property in the mode proposed by the bill; but I am here arguing upon the supposition of its being effectually executed.

nomically in supplying the market with labour, by means of the rates; but from the mode in which these rates were collected, he would receive a very large subscription towards this supply from persons not directly using the commodity when produced. In both points of view, therefore, it would be advantageous to him considerably to extend the operation of the Poor Laws.||

It has been observed by Dr. Adam Smith, that no effects of the legislature had been able to raise the salary of curates to that price which seemed necessary for their decent maintenance; and the reason which he justly assigns is, that the bounties held out to the profession by the scholarships and fellowships of the universities always occasioned a redundant supply. In the same manner if a more than usual supply of labour were encouraged by the premiums of small tenements, nothing could prevent a great and general fall in its price.

The evil would indeed ultimately check itself, as most evils do; but if we advert to the manner in which this would be done, the state to which the country must be previously reduced will not appear to be an enviable one. I apprehend that the increase would continue, till from the failure in the supply of tenements, and the diminished demand for labour, the situ-||ation of the poor supported by parishes became so uncomfortable as to deter the rising generation from marrying, with a certainty of being reduced to the same state. And if before this relaxation in the rate of increase had taken place, one third, or one half of the entire population were dependent on the parish, which would be by no means impossible, the picture of the state of society could not but be considered as a disgrace to the British constitution.

It might be imagined that the diminished demand for labour would check the increase of the labouring poor long before it had arrived at the point here supposed, but it should be recollected, that the demand for labour would extend with its reduced price, and the same quantity of capital would be able to employ a greater number of hands; at least if no difficulties were to occur in our importations of foreign corn. If the poor would continue to||receive the bounties of the rich, I apprehend that it would be possible to reduce the wages of labour to what was sufficient for the support of a single man.

I am perfectly convinced that there is scarcely any man in the kingdom who would more strongly deprecate the consequences that I have described than yourself; but you have made no provision to obviate them.

You have stated in your Bill that the parish poor in many places are very ill accommodated with habitations, and I have no doubt of the fact; but if I rightly comprehend the laws which regulate the progress of population, whatever accommodations you may make for them at present, the difficulty will shortly recur, and the only question is, whether it is better for the permanent happiness of the poor that this difficulty should exist when one eighth, or one|| seventh of the population is dependent, than when one third or one half has been reduced to the same undesirable state. I would never wish, as I have before repeatedly stated, to push general principles too far, though I think they should always be kept in view. If our poor laws continue, our accommodations for the poor must be made to keep pace with the progress of population; but as we find even under the present difficulties with regard to habitations, that the proportion of the dependent poor to the whole mass has been increasing; we may reasonably conclude that the powers which parishes at present possess for this purpose are generally speaking sufficient; and we should hesitate before we introduce so great an alteration as to make it the interest of landlords and parishes, to encourage rather than repress the increase of the dependent poor.

There is one very just apprehension with regard to the effect of the parish cottages, which||you have yourself expressed; but the cause of it is not sufficiently removed by your Bill. You recommend that these tenements should be let at the highest rents that are offered, in order that the property of those landlords who have cottages on their estates may not be materially injured by an unfair competition. But as the parishes must have a discretionary power in letting their cottages, and are indeed expressly permitted, if they see reason, to allow of their being inhabited without rent; it does not appear to me that it will be possible to keep up the rents of these cottages to their necessary, or, as Dr. Smith calls it, their natural rates; and the landholders being thus completely discouraged from building fresh cottages, or perhaps even from repairing their old ones, we should in time see the greater part of our villages consisting of parish tenements, as well as the greater part of our labouring classes dependent on parish relief.||

I need not, I am sure, insist that such a state of things, were it to take place, would completely counteract the spirit and intention of all the regulations which you have proposed. A state of dependence so general would depress the character of the common people of this country more than any system of education could elevate it; and both the power and the will to save and acquire property, would be so far diminished, that very few, I conceive, would either be disposed, or be able to make use, of your benevolent institution of the Poor's Fund, or even to become members of Friendly Societies.

I am fully aware that the poor's rates, as they are at present distributed, press most unequally on a particular class of the community; and I should think it a point of no considerable importance in the actual state of the country, to relieve the land from bearing almost exclusively||the burden of a tax, which, as it falls not only on the net rents of the landlord but in part on the capital employed in agriculture, must necessarily impede the progress of cultivation. But till some effectual and satisfactory provision can be made against the danger that I have pointed out, I should greatly fear, that in endeavouring to avoid one evil, we might fall into another far more fatal and extensive in its consequences.

Could such a provision indeed be made, the principal objection to the Poor Laws would be done away. If we could be secure, that, though the number of the dependent poor might increase with the increasing population, yet that their *proportion* to it would remain the same; and if this proportion were not so great as very materially to affect the whole body, the question would at once assume a different form. It would still be true however that the Poor Laws even in such a state||would have a tendency to depress the independent labourer, to weaken in some degree the springs of industry and good conduct, and to put virtue and vice more on a level than they would be in the natural course of things; but as in all human institutions it is impossible to avoid some disadvantages, it might fairly be urged that the certain relief of the aged and the helpless, of those who had met with misfortunes which no common prudence could have avoided, and of those who had a greater number of children than they could be expected to foresee, would more than counterbalance those inconveniences, and that the good would preponderate over the evil. I had certainly much rather that the poor were deterred from very early and improvident marriages by the fear of dependent poverty than by the contemplation of positive distress; but this concession implies that a dependent poverty is so undesirable, that if it involved a large portion of the society, the evil would entirely overwhelm the good.||

To make the advantages of a system of Poor Laws counterbalance its disadvantages, it seems to be necessary that they should be so confined in their operation, as not to depress the wages of labour below what is sufficient for the support of the *average* number of children that might be expected from each marriage. If they extended no further than this, every man in marrying might have a fair and rational hope, that by industry and good conduct, he might be able to continue independent; and if this hope failed merely through the largeness of his family, he would not be much degraded either in his own eyes or those of his fellow labourers; but should this hope be once entirely removed, should this stimulus to industry and prudence be done away, and a large proportion of births and marriages be really produced by the extension of the system (as it is physically impossible for the natural and acquired resources of any country long to support an unrestricted||population), we should soon see a most unfavourable change take place in the present small mortality, which we justly consider as one of the great tests of our national happiness; and a large proportion of deaths would invariably accompany the large proportion of births. The births however might still exceed the deaths, the population might still be increasing, but the character of it would be greatly changed; it would consist of a much larger proportion of persons not capable of adding by their exertions to the resources of the state; each generation would pass away in a more rapid succession; and the greatness of the mortality would sufficiently indicate the misery of the state of the society.

I am really unable to suggest any provision which would effectually secure us against an approach to the evils here contemplated, and not be open to the objection of violating our promises to the poor. Certainly no such provision is to be found in the clauses or probable||operation of your Bill. It is your object, and I trust that of the nation, to diminish the proportion of dependent poverty, and not to increase it; but the specific evil which I fear from your bill, as it stands at present, is an increase of it.

I should most earnestly recommend, that, at all events, one or other of the two Clauses which I have particularly noticed should be given up. If parishes be empowered to build cottages, the rates should continue on the land as the only adequate check to their increase. Or if all capital be made rateable, no new power of building tenements should be given to parishes, but every thing be left as before to individual interest and exertion.

It would certainly be most desirable to improve the cottages of the poor throughout the kingdom; and no mode of active beneficence could be pointed out to the proprietors of land,||in which they could confer so essential a benefit on the labouring poor and on the country in general, as by paying particular attention to the neatness, convenience, and substantial repairs of all the cottages on their estates. But any general plan for building cottages at the public expence, unless confined to the accommodation of a particular class of persons, or in some other way most strictly limited, is so liable to abuse, that I should be greatly afraid of seeing it attempted.

The clause which allows parishes to obtain assistance from the county stock when their rates amount to double the general average, appears to me objectionable on the same grounds, as the two Clauses just noticed. Though it might sometimes afford a relief much wanted, yet, as it would tend on the whole to make parishes more indifferent about the increase of their dependent poor, I should fear that it would produce more harm than good.||It would appear from the different prices of labour in different parishes, and the different proportions of population relieved, that the farmers, although they bear themselves a large portion of the assessments, have already learned in some places to prefer low wages and high rates, to low rates and high wages[5]. The consequences of this preference I am inclined to believe would have been more marked than they really are, if the demand for men, on account of the war, had not rendered it extremely difficult to keep down the price of labour. But as it is, this circumstance, com-||bined with the different proportions of the rack rentals on which the rates are levied, occasions so great a difference in the nominal poundage, that counties would have frequent applications from parishes that had no just claims; and it may be doubted whether the discretionary power vested in the justices would be a sufficient check to them.

I shall not detain you long on the other parts of the Bill.

You already know how ardently I wish you success in your plan of extending the benefits of educa-

---

[5] Mr. Rose, in a note to his "Observations on the Poor Laws," p. 14, says "There is but too much reason to believe "that in many parts of England the cultivators of the land "are more solicitous to restrain the price of labour than "to keep down the poor's rate; in which case the latter in "fact becomes a part of the former. In Sussex, an agri-"cultural country, the parishioners relieved are 23 in 100 "on the population, and the rates average 1*l.* 5*s.* 11½*d.* on "it; in Surrey 13 in 100, and 13*s.* 3½*d.*; in Kent 14 in 100, "and 16*s.* 7¼*d.*; and in Hants 15 in 100, and 16*s.* 3*d.*"

tion to the poor. There are at this time, I believe, few countries in Europe in which the peasantry are so ignorant as in England and Ireland; and if you are instrumental in removing this reproach, you will have just reason to be proud of your exertions. Our formidable neighbour certainly does not||think that education is likely to impede his subjects either in fighting or working; and the conduct of the conscripts, a large portion of whom is taken from a superior class of society to that which forms the mass of modern armies, clearly justifies his opinion. The principal objections which I have ever heard advanced against the education of the poor would be removed if it became general. A man who can read and write now may be discontented with his condition, and wish to rise above it; but if all his fellow-labourers possessed the same advantage, his relative situation in society would remain the same as before, and the only effect would be that the condition of the whole mass would be elevated and improved!

In the fear that any great expences in the first erection of schools should indispose the country gentlemen to the whole system, I should recommend all practicable economy in||providing proper rooms; and if each child paid a fixed sum (of course very low, and discharged by the rates in the case of orphans and parish poor), the schoolmaster would then have a stronger interest to increase the number of his pupils; and the objectionable clause might be removed, which gives a discretionary power to the parish of determining the sum to be paid, with reference to the ability of the parents. To give respectability to the schools, it would be very desireable that those who are a little above the class of labourers, should send their children to them, which they would never do, if they paid in proportion to their superior means. The due exercise of such a discretionary power would, besides, be extremely difficult; and it could hardly be expected to take place, without often producing just cause of offence.

Respecting the clause which relates to the||Poor's Fund, I see the force of your objections to country establishments, though it must be acknowledged that their vicinity to the poor man would be a very convenient and encouraging circumstance to him. It is most certainly true, as you have stated, that a secure place, in which the savings of industry might be deposited advantageously, is a want very generally felt by the poor, particularly by servants; and if this want cannot be removed in the way that they would like best, it is earnestly to be hoped, that an establishment in London, though less attractive at first, will after a time gain their full confidence.

All persons will, I conceive, agree with you in the propriety of exempting from the rates cottages, the rents of which are under five pounds. The situation of the persons inhabiting such houses is peculiarly hard. They are at present not only paying a sum for the relief of others which they can ill spare from||their own necessities; but they are really subscribing towards a competition against their own earnings. They are making themselves poorer, not only by the amount of what they pay in rates, but by the amount of the reduction which the application of those rates occasions in the general wages of labour. They seem therefore to have the strongest possible claim to the exemption proposed.

The other clauses of your bill appear to me, on the whole, calculated to improve our system of poor laws; but I have not leisure at present to enter into those details which the proper consideration of them would require; nor am I qualified justly to appreciate the difficulties with which the execution of them may be attended.

The principal object of the present letter is to point out to your attention one particular danger, of which you do not seem to be suf-||ficiently aware, and against the approaches of which your Bill certainly does not provide. I am confident that, if I have succeeded in making you see the objection in the same light that I do, you will be the first to exert your abilities to remove it. That in your generous efforts to raise and improve the condition of the poor, you may meet with the fullest success is my most ardent wish. Believe me,

Sir,

With the most sincere respect,

Your most obedient humble servant,

T. ROB^{T.} MALTHUS.

P. S. I have just met with a work entitled "A Short Inquiry into the Policy, Humanity, and past Effects of the Poor Laws," which among other important matter contains the proposal of a plan for regulating the extent of their operation in future. As it requires the continuance of those inquiries into property which are considered as being so objectionable in the Income Tax, I should suppose it is not likely to be consented to; but in other respects it is less objectionable than any I have yet seen, and is certainly well worthy of your attention. I have not yet had time to read through the whole work, but from the cursory view of it I have taken, it seems to shew not only great practical knowledge, but no ordinary acquaintance with general principles. At the same time it must be observed that the opinions of the author lead directly to that species of danger to which I have endeavoured to draw your attention in this Letter; and if they were to be adopted, unaccompanied by the proposed check, I should expect from them the very worst consequences to the happiness of the lower classes of society. Although the author in general seems clearly to understand the principle of population, yet he is not sufficiently impressed with this truth; that, even putting the consideration of dependence out of the question, it is a physical impossibility to place those who are relieved by parishes permanently in a desireable state; that is, in such a state as for a young man to feel no objection to enter into it the moment that he has an inclination to marry.

Hertford,
27th March, 1807.

THE END.

A LETTER
TO THE RT. HON. LORD GRENVILLE,
OCCASIONED BY SOME OBSERVATIONS
OF HIS LORDSHIP ON THE EAST INDIA
COMPANY'S ESTABLISHMENT FOR THE
EDUCATION OF THEIR CIVIL SERVANTS

(1813)

A

LETTER

TO THE

RT. HON. LORD GRENVILLE,

OCCASIONED BY SOME

OBSERVATIONS OF HIS LORDSHIP

ON THE

EAST INDIA COMPANY'S

ESTABLISHMENT FOR THE EDUCATION

OF THEIR

CIVIL SERVANTS.

———————

BY THE REV. T. R. MALTHUS, A.M.
PROFESSOR OF HISTORY AND POLITICAL ECONOMY AT THE
EAST INDIA COLLEGE, IN HERTFORDSHIRE.

———————

LONDON:
PRINTED FOR J. JOHNSON AND CO.,
ST. PAUL'S CHURCH-YARD.
1813.

A
LETTER,
&c. &c.

MY LORD,

I WAS in the House of Lords on the evening of the 9th of this month, and heard your lordship, at the close of a very able and brilliant speech, pass a most severe censure on the East India College. Nothing can fall from your lordship in that house, of which you are so highly distinguished a member, without producing a deep impression. But I am persuaded, that, on a question so important as the education of those who are to conduct the internal administration of our Eastern Empire, your lordship would not wish that a decision should take place, on the weight of authority alone, however great. My situation, as one of the professors in the East India College, has given me the best opportunities of observing its effects on the young men who have been edu-||cated there. I own that these effects appear to me to merit a very different description from that which was given of them by your lordship; and, from your lordship's well-known candour, I am convinced that you will not only excuse

59

the liberty I take in addressing you on this subject, but feel obliged to me for furnishing any facts and statements which may assist in enabling your lordship and the public to form an impartial judgement on a question involving such deep and various interests.

I do not recollect the precise terms of expression used by your lordship in speaking of the East India College, but I think the substance of what you said on this topic, and the manner in which it was introduced, was as follows:—

The Earl of Buckinghamshire, after paying high compliments to the marquis Wellesley's enlightened views in founding an institution for the education of the Company's civil servants, having stated that he still considered the present system that had been adopted as preferable; your lordship intimated that you could not agree with the noble earl in thinking that an establishment at home, aided by a truncated establishment in India, was to be compared with the great and consistent plan of lord Wellesley; that, on the contrary, you thought the college at Hertford ought to be suppressed as a baneful||institution, which separated young persons from their friends and companions at an early age, and formed them into a class resembling an Indian caste; that the young men to be sent out to India ought to be selected from the public schools of the country, where they would learn British feelings and British habits; that this selection should be founded on good acquirements and good conduct; and should take place at an age not earlier than the usual age of leaving England from the East India College.

These were, if I recollect right, the heads of your lordship's opinions respecting the different plans for improving the education of those who were to conduct the civil administration of India.

In considering these different plans, it will be proper first to state the origin and object of the system now actually in existence, the manner in which it has been conducted, and the degree in which it has already answered, or may be made to answer, the ends which it has in view.

Your lordship is too sound a statesman to propose the abolition of an existing establishment, unless it can be clearly made out that it was either ill planned, or has been ill executed; and that the proposed substitutes hold out a fair and rational prospect of more beneficial results.||

The continued extension of the British empire in the East, and the policy adopted for its internal administration, has, for many years, been making a great change in the qualifications necessary for its civil servants. The system of confiding the immediate exercise of every branch and department of the government to Europeans educated in its own service, commenced just previous to the arrival of the marquis Cornwallis in India; and the extension and improvement of this system, under his administration, together with the separation of the financial and judicial departments, necessarily increased the proportion of official situations, in which both general ability and a knowledge of the languages were indispensable requisites. I have learnt from good authority, that Lord Cornwallis found considerable difficulty in filling these important situations with proper persons. Many of the older civil servants were passed over in the search for the qualifications required; and, even with the greatest range that the rules of the service would admit, the search was not always successful. In short, though no written documents, I believe, remain on the subject, on account of no specific remedy having been proposed, it is known, that lord Cornwallis sensibly felt a deficiency in the education and qualifications of a great propor-||tion of the Company's servants for the offices of increasing importance and responsibility, which they were called upon to discharge.

At a subsequent period, your lordship is well aware that the penetrating eye of the marquis Wellesley saw this deficiency in so strong a light, that he thought himself imperiously called upon, as governor-general, to provide a remedy for it. For this purpose, he projected, and in part executed, a very extensive collegiate establishment at Fort William, the object of which was, to combine the usual studies of a European university with a knowledge of the oriental languages. He sent home, at the same time, a Minute in Council, dated August 18,1800, drawn up with very great ability, in which he gives a most masterly view, first, of the gradual change which has taken place in the number, importance, and responsibility of the trusts confided to the civil servants of the Company, and the high qualifications necessary to fulfil them: Secondly, of the actual deficiency in these qualifications among a considerable proportion of persons in the service, owing to an erroneous or inadequate education; and the impossibility of obtaining the education required from any system of instruction then existing, either in Europe or India. And, thirdly, of the plan by which he proposed to remedy the defects in the condition of|| the civil service; and of the beneficial results which might be expected to be derived from the collegiate establishment which he had just formed.

On some points, in the last of these divisions, I should not be able entirely to agree with the noble marquis. But in the two first divisions the arguments appear to me quite unanswerable. They are, probably, familiar to your lordship but, from the culpable in-attention to Indian subjects in the British public, they have not been so widely circulated as they ought to have been; and I know your lordship will excuse my making a few extracts from them, in the hope that they may by chance meet the view of some persons who have not seen the Minute.

After stating the various and arduous duties to be discharged by those who fill the judicial and financial departments in the civil administration of India, and the superior qualifications which were desirable even in the commercial department, the marquis goes on to say: "The civil servants of the English East India Company, therefore, can no longer be considered as the agents of a *commercial concern*; they are, in fact, the ministers and officers of a *powerful sovereign*; they must now be viewed in that capacity with a reference not to their nominal, but to their real occupations. They are required to||discharge the functions of mag-istrates, judges, ambassadors, and governors of prov-inces, in all the complicated and extensive relations of those sacred trusts and exalted stations, and under peculiar circumstances, which greatly enhance the solemnity of every public obligation, and aggravate the difficulty of every public charge. Their duties are those of statesmen in every other part of the world, with no other characteristic differences than the obstacles opposed by an unfavourable climate, a foreign language, the peculiar usages and laws of India, and the manners of its inhabitants. Their studies, the discipline of their education, their habits of life, their manners and morals, should therefore be so ordered and regulated, as to establish a just conformity between their personal consideration and the dignity and importance of their public stations, and a sufficient correspondence between their qualifications and their duties. Their education should be *founded* in a general knowledge of those branches of literature and science, which form the basis of the education of persons destined to similar occupations in Europe," &c.: and to this foundation should be added the studies more particularly appropriate to their situations in India.

In reference to the qualifications and studies above described, lord Wellesley proceeds "to||review the course through which the junior civil servants of the East India Company now enter upon the important duties of their respective stations, to consider whether they now possess, or can attain the means of qualifying themselves sufficiently for those stations, and to examine whether the great body of the civil servants of the East India Company, at any of the presidencies, can now be deemed competent to discharge their arduous and comprehensive trusts in a manner correspondent to the interests and honour of the British name in India, or to the prosperity and happiness of our native subjects."

The result of this examination shows a deficiency of the qualifications required by the service; and this deficiency is attributed by his lordship, partly to a mercantile education in Europe; partly to the premature interruption of a proper course of instruction; and partly to the numerous disadvantages and dangers to which the junior servants of the Company are exposed during the early period of their residence in India. "It has been justly observed," says lord Wellesley, "that all the merits of the civil servants are to be ascribed to their own character, talents, and exertions, while their defects must be imputed to the constitution and practice of the service, which have not been accommodated to the progressive||changes of our situation in India, and have not kept pace with the growth of this empire, or with the increasing extent and importance of the functions and duties of the civil service. The study and acquisition of the languages have however been extended to Bengal; and the general knowledge and qualifications of the civil servants have been improved: the proportion of the civil servants in Bengal who have made a considerable progress towards the attainment of the qualifications requisite in their several stations, appears great, and even astonishing, when viewed with regard to the early disadvantages, embarrassments and defects of the civil service. But this proportion will appear very different, when compared with the exigencies of the state, with the magnitude of these provinces, and with the total number of the civil servants which must apply the succession to the great offices of the government. *It must be admitted that the great body of the civil servants in Bengal is not at present sufficiently qualified to discharge the duties of the several arduous stations in the administration of this empire; and that it is peculiarly deficient in the judicial, fiscal, financial, and political branches of the government. . . . . .*

"If the good government of this empire be the primary duty of its sovereign, it must ever||be a leading branch of that duty to facilitate to the public officers and ministers the means of qualifying themselves for their respective functions: the efficiency of the service cannot be wisely or conscientiously left to depend upon the success of individual or accidental merit struggling against the defects of established institutions, operating in a regular, uninterrupted course, upon the various characters, talents, and acquirements of individuals. The nature of our establishments should furnish fixed and systematic encouragement to animate, to facilitate, to reward, the progress of industry and virtue, and fixed and systematic discipline, to repress and correct the excesses of contrary dispositions.

"From these remarks may be deduced the indispensable necessity of providing some speedy and effectual remedy for the improvement of the education of the young men destined to the civil service in India."

This education, the marquis says, should be neither exclusively European nor Indian, but of a mixed nature. "Its foundation must be judiciously laid in

England, and the superstructure systematically completed in India."

These, and other views, most ably detailed in the Minute, determined the governor-general to found an extensive collegiate institution at Fort William, in which all the writers, on their||first arrival in India, were to be received; and the course of study, previous to their leaving it, was to be fixed at three years.

With regard to the period of their arrival in India, it is observed, that "the junior civil servants must continue to embark for India at the age of fifteen or sixteen, that they may be tractable instruments in the hands of the government; that their morals and habits may be formed with proper safeguards against the peculiar nature of the views, and characteristic dangers of Indian society; that they may be able to pass through the service before the vigor of life has ceased, and to return with a competent fortune to Europe, while the affections and attachments, which bind them to their native country, continue to operate with full force."

The collegiate establishment thus founded, it is well known, was not sanctioned by the Court of Directors in its full extent. The main ground of their rejection of it, they state to be, the enormous expense in which it must involve the Company, which they consider as too great for the actual state of its affairs. They pay high compliments to the liberal and enlightened spirit and great ability of the marquis, though they only express their approbation of parts of his plan. They acknowledge, however, the necessity of an improved education for their civil||servants, but seem to think that this object might be effectually accomplished by an enlarged seminary for oriental learning at Calcutta, combined with an improved system of education in Europe, suitable to the sphere of life in which their civil servants are intended to move.

It was for the specific purpose of securing such an improved education to their civil servants before they leave England, without detaining them till the usual age at which an university course finishes, to which detention the marquis had objected, that the Court of Directors founded the institution in Hertfordshire.

At this institution, the students commence a course of more general instruction than is to be found at schools, at the same period that they were to commence it in India, according to lord Wellesley's plan, and yet proceed to their destination at eighteen or nineteen, an age at which the constitution is supposed to be better fortified against the Indian climate than two or three years earlier; and yet not sufficiently advanced to be open to those objections urged by lord Wellesley against a detention till twenty-one or twenty-two.

In the East India College, so constituted, the plan upon which the system of instruction is conducted seems to be well calculated to answer||the end which it has in view. Every young man, before his admission into the college, is required to produce a testimonial from his schoolmaster, and to pass an examination in Greek, Latin, and arithmetic, before the principal and professors, sufficient to ascertain his having previously received the usual school education of a gentleman. The lectures of the different professors in the college are given in a manner to make previous preparation invariably necessary, and to encourage most effectually habits of industry and application. In their substance, they embrace the important subjects of classical literature, the oriental languages, the elements of mathematics and natural philosophy, the laws of England, general history, and political economy.

At the commencement of the institution, it was feared by some persons that this variety would too much distract the attention of students at the age of sixteen or seventeen, and prevent them from making a satisfactory progress in any department; but instances of distinguished success, in many of these studies at the same time, have proved that these fears were without foundation, and that this variety has not only been useful to them in rendering a methodical arrangement of their hours of study more necessary, but has decidedly con-||tributed to enlarge, invigorate and mature their understandings.

It was also imagined that some of the pursuits which contribute to form this variety, were of too difficult a nature for young men of the age above mentioned; and the subject of political economy was considered as one. I confess that I once thought so myself. But the particular examples, which I have witnessed, of distinguished progress in this study at the East India College, and the numerous instances of very fair progress, enable me to say, with confidence, that a youth of seventeen, (and this is the most usual age at which the study is begun, as it is generally confined to the last year or year and a half,) with a good understanding, is fully able to comprehend the principles of political economy, and is rarely inclined to think them either too difficult or too dull to engage his attention.

On all the important subjects above enumerated, examinations take place twice in the year, at the end of each term. These examinations last above a fortnight. They are conducted upon the plan of the great public and collegiate examinations in the universities, particularly in that of Cambridge, with such further improvements as experience has suggested. The questions given are framed with a view to as-||certain the degree of progress and actual proficiency in each particular department, on the subjects studied during the preceding term; and the answers are, in all cases which will admit of it, given in writing, in the presence of the professors, and without the possibility of a reference to books. After the examination in any particular department is over, the professor in that department reviews at his leisure all the papers which he has received, and places, as nearly as he can, each individual in the numerical order of his relative merit, and in certain divisions, implying his degree of positive merit. These arrangements are all subject to the controul of the whole collegiate body. They repair considerable time and attention, and are executed with scrupulous care, and, I firmly believe, with singular impartiality. If the lists of many successive years were examined with the most scrutinizing eye, I doubt if the slightest trace of general connexion could be found, between the places of the students in these examinations, and the rank or supposed influence of their patrons.

Besides the classifications above mentioned, medals,

prizes of books, and honorary distinctions, are awarded to those who are the heads of classes, or as high as second, third, fourth, or fifth, in two, three, four, or five departments.||

These means of exciting emulation and industry have been attended with great success. Though there are some, unquestionably, on whom motives of this kind will not, or cannot operate, and with whom therefore little can be done; yet a more than usual proportion seem to be animated by a strong desire, accompanied by corresponding efforts, to make a distinguished progress in the various studies proposed to them. The young men, who have come to the college tolerably good scholars, have often, during their stay of two years, made such advances in the classical department as would have done them very high credit, if they had devoted to it the whole of their time; while the contemporary honours, which they obtained in other departments, sufficiently proved that their attention had not been confined to one study. And many, who have come from our public and private schools at sixteen, with such low classical attainments as to indicate a want either of capacity or application, have shown by their subsequent progress, even in the classical department, and still more by their distinguished exertions in others, that a new field and new stimulants had worked a most beneficial change in their feelings and habits, and had awakened energies and capacities, of which they were before scarcely conscious.||

There are four or five of the professors of high character in the university of Cambridge, and thoroughly conversant with its public examinations, who can take upon themselves to affirm, that they have never witnessed a greater proportion of various and successful exertion, in the whole course of their academical experience, than has appeared at the examinations in the East India College.

It may indeed, I believe, be safely asserted, that a considerable proportion of the students, who have proceeded to India from the College, have left it with more improved understandings, and with a greater quantity of useful knowledge, fitted for the early discharge of public business, than could be found among any set of young men, taken in the same way and at the same age, from any place of education in Europe; and many of them with such distinguished attainments already acquired, such means of acquiring more, and such fixed habits of honour, integrity, and good conduct, that no situation, however high, to which they could be promoted, would be above their powers or beyond their deserts.

With regard to what your lordship stated, respecting the separation of the young men who are educated for the civil service of the company, into a distinct class, resembling an||Indian caste, I cannot but think that you must have been under some misconception as to the age at which the students enter and leave the college. Your lordship has probably heard of a school connected with it, and may imagine that an exclusive system of education is pursued from the earliest youth. But, in fact, the numbers which come from this school are comparatively small; and these have always been mixed with sixty or seventy other boys entirely unconnected with India. The great body of the students come from the public and private schools of England, Scotland, and Ireland, about the age of sixteen; and their residence of two, or at the most three years, at the college, is so far from having the effect of giving them feelings and prejudices exclusively connected with India, that some of the complaints, which have been made against the college, are, that many students acquire such a taste for the European part of their education, that they do not pay sufficient attention to the oriental part; and that, by their protracted stay in England, they strengthen so much all the ties which unite them to their friends and their native country, that they are too unwilling to leave it.

In the free constitution of this country, it is surely of great importance that our officers of the army and navy should not lose the feelings||of citizens. But if it is imperiously necessary that their education should finish sooner than the usual course of school and university discipline permits, and if they are required to know certain branches of science appropriate to their professions, which are not taught in the common places of education; we do not hesitate to separate them, for a time, from other boys, trusting, and trusting I think justly, that, while they are living under the British constitution, and seeing continually their parents and friends, and hearing their conversation, they are not likely to lose the habits and feelings of British citizens.

But there is another argument, my lord, which, in reference to the opinions expressed by your lordship in the house, must be considered as of great weight. Your lordship decidedly approved of the marquis Wellesley's collegiate establishment at Fort William, or at least most decidedly preferred it to the college at home. But it was a marked feature in the marquis's plan, that the Company's writers should embark for India at fifteen or sixteen. Unless, therefore, your lordship could be certain that that part of the system would be given up, on which your noble friend lays considerable stress, consistency would require that you should argue with equal force against the establishment of a college in India, as for the suppression of the college in||England. For your lordship would hardly contend, that youths going at fifteen or sixteen to India, where, the moment they arrive, they see on all hands that they are the members of a privileged order, will not be likely to resemble more in their exclusive feelings an Indian caste, than if they had lived till eighteen or nineteen under the British constitution, and had heard, as they might do, British feelings expressed by those around them, through the whole period of their stay, although the greatest part of it were devoted to their studies in the East India College.

I cannot but think, then, my lord, that any just grounds of objection to the present system of education, for the Company's writers, on account of its exclusiveness, if they exist at all, must exist in so slight a degree, as to be entirely overbalanced by the specific advantages which it confers. And if I have been successful in stating these advantages, as they appear to my own mind, it must be allowed that the college established by the Court of Directors, in Hertfordshire, does not seem to have been either so ill planned, or so ill executed, as to require immediate suppression.

But, though I am a friend to existing establishments, I should not be so bigotted as to adhere to them, if grounds of clear and unequivocal preference could be made out in favour of others,||which were proposed to be substituted for them.

I proceed, therefore, to consider the plan of marquis Wellesley, on its extended scale, and to state some objections to it, which, after the maturest consideration, have always struck me as most formidable.

First, your lordship does not allow, that the very great expense of such an establishment was a sufficient reason for the rejection of a plan, the important object of which was the education of the statesmen of India. And in this opinion I entirely concur, if so necessary an end could not be accomplished by other means, more economical and equally efficient. But, of course, if this could be done, your lordship would allow economy to be a most just cause of preference. But, besides this consideration, an evil would be likely to arise from this expense greatly prejudicial to the main purpose of the establishment. The salaries necessary to induce men of high character and attainments, in our English universities, to afford their assistance in India, would be so great, that, though the founder of a new establishment would not hesitate to give them, it is probable that the system would not be persevered in to its due extent. And the effect would be, that persons of inferior character and attainments would be employed, and that, independently of||the climate, and other disadvantages, an Asiatic education would not, in point of instruction, bear a comparison with that of a European.

Secondly, If a regular system of discipline were established, as proposed by lord Wellesley, it would of course be necessary to maintain it by appropriate sanctions. Your lordship must be well aware, that the main support of all discipline, both in our public schools and our universities, is the power of expulsion; and, that few great boys would submit to corporal punishment at school, and few young men to impositions and confinement at the universities, if it were not that the alternative of being sent from their school or college is always ready to be applied.

In the public disputation, at the college of Fort William, in September, 1810, lord Minto alludes to three students, who in a period of three years, had made no progress in any language. He proposes to afford them the opportunity of one year more; but announces to them the resolution adopted by the college, that if, at the fourth annual examination, they had not attained the requisite proficiency in two languages, they shall be dismissed from the college, and suspended the service. In this case, the simple object before the students was a moderate proficiency in two oriental languages; and on this one object all their prospects in life||seemed to depend; and yet it appears they failed. If, on the establishment of a regular system of university education in the East, other attainments, besides two languages, were required, and if it were necessary to support, by adequate punishments, an attention to the laws and regulations of the college, it is impossible not to believe, that, among one hundred and twenty young men taken promiscuously from Europe, many failures would every year occur. And what is to be done with these unfortunate young men? They must either be sent back from India, at a great loss and expense, to the utter ruin of all their future prospects in life, and the deep distress of their families; or they must remain in India unemployed, a heavy burden on the Company's finances, though in hopeless indigence themselves; or, what is still worse, they must be employed to the manifest injury of the service, and in violation probably of the repeated pledges and promises of the government, and to the consequent destruction of the college discipline.

I own, my lord, that the difficulty of adequately enforcing obedience to a code of academical regulations in India, strikes me as so great that I see no fair prospects of its being overcome.||

But by far the greatest objection to a complete university education in India remains yet to be considered; an objection which appears to me to be at once decisive of the question. I am informed from the most undoubted authorities, that the young men, who go out as writers, have the power of borrowing almost any sum of money from particular natives who speculate on their future prospects in the service; and that this power they are too frequently inclined to exercise in the earlier part of their career, and particularly during their stay at the expensive residence of Calcutta. Your lordship is as well acquainted with the university of Oxford as I am with that of Cambridge; and I would put it fairly to your lordship's candour to say, whether these venerable places of education would be, in any respect, what they now are, in literature, in morals and in discipline, if every undergraduate had an unlimited command of money; and if, in addition to this command, he was continually beset by the temptations to indolence and sensual indulgencies, peculiar to a warm and luxurious climate, and a city nearly as large as London. It is impossible, my lord, that, with your knowledge of the human character, you should think that they would still be the same. It is impossible not to allow that, with such facilities of||borrowing and such temptations to spend, a complete university education in India would be a fearful experiment.

Nor would the failure of the college discipline be by any means the principal evil to be contemplated. The writers, who involve themselves early in considerable debts, are seldom or ever able to extricate themselves. Interest accumulates upon interest, the increasing salary is unable to discharge the increasing debt; and, not only all prospect of a return to Europe, with a competency, is for ever closed, but the honour and integrity of the persons thus embarrassed and endangered, and the service suffers in the tenderest point.

Every human system and provision must bend to circumstances. The service in India absolutely requires a certain knowledge of the oriental languages. Some residence therefore in the country, before an appointment to an official situation can with propriety take place, may be absolutely necessary; but, knowing the very serious dangers to which this period is exposed, it is unquestionably a paramount duty, in the governing power, wherever it is placed, not to protract it unnecessarily, not to expose the morals, happiness, and fortunes of the young men in their service to greater and longer con-||tinued risks than that service imperiously requires.

I come now to the consideration of the plan suggested by your lordship.

As almost all the offices in India, to be filled by the young men sent out from England, are offices of great responsibility and importance, and becoming daily more so, I should naturally be disposed to approve of that part of any plan which involved a principle of previous selection in Europe. In every country, the persons taken to conduct its civil administration, though not always, of course, well chosen, are selected from a considerable range of candidates, at an age when their competency to fill the situations for which they apply, may be fairly estimated; and when those, who are obviously disqualified, are so far behind, in the race of competition, as seldom to presume to offer themselves. It is an unusual phenomenon to see the interior government of a vast empire conducted by persons chosen from the narrow range of thirty or forty young men sent out annually to their destination, almost without any original discrimination. It must depend entirely upon the *proportion* of offices, which require great ability to those which may be discharged with little or none, whether it is possible, in the nature of things, for educa-||tion alone, without previous selection, to furnish an adequate supply of sufficiently able civil servants for India. Education will render a very much greater proportion out of a certain number competent to discharge the offices that require talents, information, and industry, but it cannot fit, either for important or only respectable stations, those who are absolutely deficient in capacity, or confirmed in habits of idleness.

Some principle of selection, therefore, I should think highly desirable, with a view to the good administration of India; but the suggestion of your lordship respecting public schools appears to me to be open to considerable objections.

In the first place, my lord, I cannot think that it would be just and fair to Scotland and Ireland, to exclude them so much from Indian prizes, as they would necessarily be excluded by this system. Nor would it, in my opinion, be fair to persons of moderate fortunes in England, particularly in the distant parts of it, to oblige them to undergo the extravagant expense of a long residence at a public school, with the mere hope of succeeding in a lottery, where the competitors would be many, and the prizes comparatively few. There are many parents, who can give their sons a good education in||their own neighbourhood, and are both able and willing to support for them, during two or three years, the expenses of the East India College, under a reasonable certainty of their proceeding to India, who would have been precluded from any chance of success upon the plan suggested by your lordship.

In one part of your lordship's speech, I think you said that you approved of the present very various distribution of the Company's patronage. Surely, the plan proposed by your lordship would be a very marked, and hardly justifiable confinement of it.

Secondly, If the age of proceeding to India were not earlier than eighteen, and yet nothing had been done at that period in commencing a university education, or laying a foundation for the oriental languages, the whole term of three years at a college in India would unquestionably be necessary to qualify a young man properly for the civil service. This delay of two or three years in the commencement of active employment, would probably delay proportionately the period of returning with a competency to Europe. And such a protracted stay, at the usual age of returning, is considered by lord Wellesley, and would be considered by most persons connected with India, as an evil of no small importance.||

Thirdly, All the difficulties attending a system of collegiate discipline in India, and all the dangers of a protracted residence at Calcutta, with an unlimitted command of money, will apply equally to your lordship's plan and that of the marquis Wellesley. There is a point too equally applicable to both, which, in considering the marquis's system, I did not sufficiently advert to; and this is, that, as the period of change from a school to a university education, is, perhaps, of all others, the most critical period of human life, and the most decisive of the future character, it is a matter of the very highest importance that this period should be passed under favourable, rather than unfavourable auspices. I cannot, however, readily conceive a more inauspicious situation for the commencement of new and difficult studies, than that of a young man on his first arrival in India, surrounded by natives devoted to his will, discouraged from application by the enfeebling effects of the climate; and beset by every temptation and novelty, which can attract his imagination, and divert his attention from serious pursuits. That these disadvantages of situation diminish after a certain period, is unquestionably true; and it is equally true that they will sometimes yield to great, and particularly to near objects, such||as that of acquiring those languages which are an immediate passport to an official appointment; but it will be allowed that they must operate as formidable discouragements, to begin a course of law, history, political economy, and natural philosophy, or to continue a course of classical studies. It was intended by lord Wellesley that a great variety of lectures, besides those in the oriental languages, should be given in the College of Fort William; and some were actually begun; but I have understood that none were attended except the languages.

If general knowledge, then, be necessary, it is quite clear, that as much of it as can be imparted in Europe, consistently with the nature of the service, should be so imparted. It may fairly be presumed that its quality will be superior; it is unquestionably much cheaper; and it is given under circumstances which render it beyond comparison more efficient.

It appears, from experience, that a university education may be very successfully begun in Europe from sixteen to eighteen; and the first steps thus taken, the first difficulties thus overcome under favourable auspices, may decide much with regard to the future tastes and habits. A young man, thus prepared, even if he relaxes his efforts, on his first arrival in India,|| will always know how to resume his literary pursuits; and, having generally collected a few books on the subjects which formed his studies in Europe, he will seldom remain long without the power and the inclination to use them.

In every point of view in which I can consider this subject, it appears to me highly advantageous, if it be possible, to secure the commencement of a university education in Europe, and highly disadvantageous to leave it to the first two or three years of Indian residence.

But, fourthly, the most weighty practical objection to your lordship's plan, remains yet to be considered. It takes for granted, that the East India Company's charter will not be renewed. But, as in the present temper both of his Majesty's government and of the Company, there is every reason to believe that it will be renewed, your lordship's observations do not apply to the actual state of things. These observations were indeed made, if I recollect, chiefly upon the supposition of the administration of India falling to the government of this country, and of its being necessary on that account, (and I think it would be imperiously necessary,) to break down the Indian patronage in such a manner as to prevent it from destroying the balance of the British constitution. In this point of view the suggestions of your lord-||ship were of high value, and, with some modifications, might be adopted with great advantage; but they appear to me to furnish no plan for securing an improved education to the civil servants in India, which can reasonably be expected to be put in execution on the renewal of the Company's charter—an event of which there is little reason to doubt.

Under all the circumstances of the case, therefore, it will not, I think, appear, that the Court of Directors were wrong, in endeavouring to supply the acknowledged want of an improved education for their civil servants, by an appropriate establishment at home. In doing this, they did not of course imagine, that by any magic they could give as complete an education to young men of eighteen, as might be obtained by those of twenty-one, after a regular course of instruction at the best of our public schools and a completion of their course of study at Oxford or Cambridge. Nor did they imagine that the oriental languages could be taught with the same ease and expedition at any institution in England, as in the country in which these languages are spoken. But they had learnt from experience that it was highly desirable that their writers should go out from England as nearly as eighteen or nineteen; and they had learnt from experience, that a long|| residence at Calcutta was likely to be attended with the most fatal consequences. They hoped and expected therefore by commencing a university education rather sooner than usual, and abridging its duration, they might still be able to communicate a better system of European instruction than could be accomplished in India; and, by uniting with it a foundation of the oriental languages, and allowing almost the whole attention to be directed to this one object during the first year of Indian residence, they might reduce, perhaps to one-third, the necessary period of stay in Calcutta previous to an appointment. And, in these hopes and expectations, they have not been, in my opinion, deceived. I feel no doubt that the European part of the education given at the East India College has been more effective, and better, in every point of view, than that which could be given in India. And experience has proved that, with a good foundation of the oriental languages, and the vigorous habits of application acquired at the college, a considerable proportion of the students who have left it have been able to qualify themselves for official appointments in less than a single year's residence at Calcutta[1]. Already, I am informed, it has||been acknowledged at the different presidencies in India, that

---

[1] In the year ending June, 1811, the only year of which all the required particulars can as yet be collected, the number of students which left the Calcutta college qualified for employment was twenty, of whom the number from the college in Hertfordshire was twelve; *viz.*

Six, who left the Calcutta college, after 6 months residence.
Two, ... after 8 months residence.
One, ... after 9 months residence.
One, ... after 2 years residence.
Two, ... after 3 years residence.

The number of students who left the Calcutta college at the same time, but who never were at the college in Hertfordshire, was eight; *viz.*

Three, after a residence of 2¾ years.
One, ... of 3 years.
One, ... of 3¾ years.
Two, ... of 4 years.
One, ... of 4½ years.

The efficacy of the establishment in England, in abridging the period of study in the college of Calcutta, can scarcely be questioned after this statement.

a marked improvement has been observed in the conduct and attainments of the young men who have arrived since the establishment of the college in England; and it has been distinctly stated by lord Minto that the period of residence at the College of Fort William dependent upon a proficiency in two oriental languages, is decidedly shortened.

Yet whatever the East India College in England has hitherto done, has been done under great and obvious disadvantages—disadvantages sufficient to undermine the discipline of any||place of education, particularly that of a new institution uncongenial to the prevailing prejudices of the public.

It has had to contend with the evil of an appeal, in all cases of importance, to a body of men, whose individual interests could hardly fail to be always in opposition to the interests of the discipline. It has had to contend with a party connected with Indian affairs, from the first, decidedly hostile to the college, and indulging themselves, as there is too much reason to believe, in a sort of language respecting it, of a nature to produce the very worst effects on the temper and conduct of the students connected with them. And it has had to contend with an impression of instability, arising from the two preceding causes, necessarily tending to generate disturbances, and to produce the very evils which it prognosticates.

But let these disadvantages be removed, let the discipline be placed on a proper footing, by giving full powers to the Principal and Professors, with an appeal only to some one individual of high rank, not immediately connected with the patronage of the students.

Let the stability of the college be secured by some legislative sanction, which will prevent it from depending upon the variable wills of a fluctuating body of Directors. Let the age of admission be sixteen, instead of fifteen. Let||some moderate test be established, particularly in the oriental languages, to stimulate the industry of the most idle and least able students, and to prevent those from proceeding to India who can only be a burden to the service. And, to these, let a few subordinate improvements be added, which need not be detailed here: and I should be very much deceived, if the institution did not answer the express purpose for which it was established, in a more than common degree.

I earnestly entreat your lordship, then, to reconsider what you have said on this subject. Recollect, my lord, that this is not a question about the general merits of public or private education. It has nothing to do with any general innovation in the modes of instruction to be recommended in this country. It is one of those practical questions, which must often come before a statesman—how to accomplish a particular object in the best manner—how to supply a particular want most effectually, as well as most economically. In the consideration of such a question, it is impossible to form a correct judgement by taking only one view of it. A public school and three year's residence at one of our universities may be decidedly the best education for an English statesman; but for an Indian statesman, who must be acquainted with the oriental languages, and habituated to Indian customs and manners before he loses his pliability, there is evidently||not time for such a course. The oriental languages are best taught in the East; but languages alone are not a sufficient qualification for the administration of the British government in India, and general knowledge is best taught in the west. The advantages of an Indian career, commencing at fifteen, with a view to an early return to Europe, is counterbalanced by a weaker constitution, feebler European feelings and attachments, and inferior European information. While the disadvantages of a protracted stay in Europe and a later return, may be compensated by a constitution better able to bear the climate, and a degree of European knowledge and feeling better calculated to infuse a spirit of British justice into a government over sixty millions of Asiatics. In short, whatever decision is formed, it must be a compromise between various and contending difficulties. And amidst this conflict of opposite views, I am strongly inclined to suspect that a common school education till sixteen, with an early university education in Europe till eighteen or nineteen, accompanied by instructions in the oriental languages, is the best compromise that can be adopted; that is, that it unites the greatest number of advantages with the fewest disadvantages; which in a case of this kind is the only rational foundation for a decision.

With these impressions, my lord, it must be||my opinion that the East India College is a beneficial institution, and is actually supplying that want of an improved education for the civil servants of the Company, so clearly stated by lord Wellesley. This opinion I am confident that I should hold, if I had not the slightest connexion with the college, provided I possessed the same means of information which I do at present, and had my attention directed in the same manner to this particular subject.

I am compelled therefore to think that, if the effect of your lordship's speech should be to weaken the efficiency, or ultimately to destroy the present establishment, without absolutely securing to the country the means of supplying to its eastern dominions a better system of education in its stead, your lordship will most unintentionally have done a serious injury to the interests of good government in India.

I am, my lord,
With the highest respect,
Your lordship's very obedient,
Humble servant,
T. R. MALTHUS.

OBSERVATIONS ON THE EFFECTS

OF THE CORN LAWS

(SECOND EDITION, 1814)

OBSERVATIONS

ON THE

EFFECTS

OF THE

C O R N   L A W S,

AND OF A

RISE OR FALL IN THE PRICE OF CORN

ON THE

AGRICULTURE

AND

GENERAL WEALTH OF THE COUNTRY.

BY THE REV. T. R. MALTHUS,

PROFESSOR OF POLITICAL ECONOMY AT THE EAST INDIA
COLLEGE, HERTFORDSHIRE.

SECOND EDITION.

LONDON:
PRINTED FOR J. JOHNSON AND CO.
ST. PAUL'S CHURCH-YARD.
1814.

OBSERVATIONS,

&c. &c.

A REVISION of the Corn Laws, it is understood, is immediately to come under the consideration of the legislature. That the decision on such a subject, should be founded on a correct and enlightened view of the whole question, will be allowed to be of the utmost importance, both with regard to the stability of the measures to be adopted, and the effects to be expected from them.

For an attempt to contribute to the stock of information necessary to form such a decision, no apology can be necessary. It may seem indeed probable, that but little further light can be thrown on a subject, which, owing to the system adopted in this country, has been so frequently the topic of discussion; but, after the best consideration which I have been able to give it, I own, it appears to me, that some important considerations have been neglected on||
both sides of the question, and that the effects of the Corn Laws, and of a rise or fall in the price of corn, on the agriculture and general wealth of the state, have not yet been fully laid before the public.

If this be true, I cannot help attributing it in some

degree to the very peculiar argument brought forward by Dr. Smith, in his discussion of the bounty upon the exportation of corn. Those who are conversant with the "Wealth of Nations," will be aware, that its great author has, on this occasion, left entirely in the background the broad, grand, and almost unanswerable arguments, which the general principles of political economy furnish in abundance against all systems of bounties and restrictions, and has only brought forwards, in a prominent manner, one which, it is intended, should apply to corn alone.

It is not surprising that so high an authority should have had the effect of attracting the attention of the advocates of each side of the question, in an especial manner, to this particular argument. Those who have maintained the same cause with Dr. Smith, have treated it nearly in the same way; and, though they may have alluded to the other more general and legitimate arguments against bounties and restrictions, have almost universally seemed to place||their chief reliance on the appropriate and particular argument relating to the nature of corn.

On the other hand, those who have taken the opposite side of the question, if they have imagined, that they had combated this particular argument with success, have been too apt to consider the point as determined, without much reference to the more weighty and important arguments, which remained behind.

Among the latter description of persons I must rank myself. I have always thought, and still think, that this peculiar argument of Dr. Smith, is fundamentally erroneous, and that it cannot be maintained without violating the great principles of supply and demand, and contradicting the general spirit and scope of the reasonings, which pervade the "Wealth of Nations."

But I am most ready to confess, that, on a former occasion, when I considered the Corn Laws, my attention was too much engrossed by this one peculiar view of the subject, to give the other arguments, which belong to it, their due weight.

I am anxious to correct an error, of which I feel conscious. It is not however my intention, on the present occasion, to express an opinion on the general question. I shall only endeavour to state, with the strictest impartiality, what appear to me to be the advantages and disadvan-||tages of each system, in the actual circumstances of our present situation, and what are the specific consequences, which may be expected to result from the adoption of either. My main object is to assist in affording the materials for a just and enlightened decision; and, whatever that decision may be, to prevent disappointment, in the event of the effects of the measure not being such as were previously contemplated. Nothing would tend so powerfully to bring the general principles of political economy into disrepute, and to prevent their spreading, as their being supported upon any occasion by reasoning, which constant and unequivocal experience should afterwards prove to be fallacious.

We must begin, therefore, by an inquiry into the truth of Dr. Smith's argument, as we cannot with propriety proceed to the main question, till this preliminary point is settled.

The substance of his argument is, that corn is of so peculiar a nature, that its real price cannot be raised by an increase of its money-price; and that, as it is clearly an increase of real price alone, which can encourage its production, the rise of money-price, occasioned by a bounty, can have no such effect.

It is by no means intended to deny the powerful influence of the price of corn upon the price of labour, on an average of a considerable num-||ber of years; but that this influence is not such as to prevent the movement of capital to, or from the land, which is the precise point in question, will be made sufficiently evident by a short inquiry into the manner in which labour is paid and brought into the market, and by a consideration of the consequences to which the assumption of Dr. Smith's proposition would inevitably lead.

In the first place, if we inquire into the expenditure of the labouring classes of society, we shall find, that it by no means consists wholly in food, and still less, of course, in mere bread or grain. In looking over that mine of information, for every thing relating to prices and labour, Sir Frederick Morton Eden's Work on the Poor, I find, that in a labourer's family of about an average size, the articles of house-rent, fuel, soap, candles, tea, sugar, and clothing, are generally equal to the articles of bread or meal. On a very rough estimate, the whole may be divided into five parts, of which two consist of meal or bread, two of the articles above mentioned, and one of meat, milk, butter, cheese, and potatoes. These divisions are, of course, subject to considerable variations, arising from the number of the family, and the amount of the earnings. But if they merely approximate towards the truth, a rise in the price of corn must be both slow and partial|| in its effects upon labour. Meat, milk, butter, cheese, and potatoes are slowly affected by the price of corn. House-rent, bricks, stone, timber, fuel, soap, candles, and clothing, still more slowly; and, as far as some of them depend, in part or in the whole, upon foreign materials (as is the case with leather, linen, cottons, soap, and candles), they may be considered as independent of it; like the two remaining articles of tea and sugar, which are by no means unimportant in their amount.

It is manifest therefore that the whole of the wages of labour can never rise and fall in proportion to the variations in the price of grain. And that the effect produced by these variations, whatever may be its amount, must be very slow in its operation, is proved by the manner in which the supply of labour takes place; a point, which has been by no means sufficiently attended to.

Every change in the prices of commodities, if left to find their natural level, is occasioned by some change, actual or expected, in the state of the demand or supply. The reason why the consumer pays a tax upon any manufactured commodity, or an advance in the price of any of its component parts, is because, if he cannot or will not pay this advance of price, the commodity will not be supplied in the same quantity as||before; and the next year there will only be such a proportion in the market, as is accommodated to the number of persons who will consent to pay the tax.

But, in the case of labour, the operation of withdrawing the commodity is much slower and more painful. Although the purchasers refuse to pay the advanced price, the same supply will necessarily remain in the market, not only the next year, but for some years to come. Consequently, if no increase take place in the demand, and the advanced price of provisions be not so great, as to make it obvious that the labourer cannot support his family, it is probable, that he will continue to pay this advance, till a relaxation in the rate of the increase of population causes the market to be under-supplied with labour; and then, of course, the competition among the purchasers will raise the price above the proportion of the advance, in order to restore the supply. In the same manner, if an advance in the price of labour has taken place during two or three years of great scarcity, it is probable that, on the return of plenty, the real recompence of labour will continue higher than the usual average, till a too rapid increase of population causes a competition among the labourers, and a consequent diminution of the price of labour below the usual rate.||

This account of the manner in which the price of corn may be expected to operate upon the price of labour, according to the laws which regulate the progress of population, evidently shews, that corn and labour rarely keep an even pace together; but must often be separated at a sufficient distance and for a sufficient time, to change the direction of capital.

As a further confirmation of this truth, it may be useful to consider, secondly, the consequences to which the assumption of Dr. Smith's proposition would inevitably lead.

If we suppose, that the real price of corn is unchangeable, or not capable of experiencing a relative increase or decrease of value, compared with labour and other commodities, it will follow, that agriculture is at once excluded from the operation of that principle, so beautifully explained and illustrated by Dr. Smith, by which capital flows from one employment to another, according to the various and necessarily fluctuating wants of society. It will follow, that the growth of corn has, at all times, and in all countries, proceeded with a uniform unvarying pace, occasioned only by the equable increase of agricultural capital, and can never have been accelerated, or retarded, by variations of demand. It will follow, that if a country happened to be either overstocked or understocked with corn,||no motive of interest could exist for withdrawing capital from agriculture, in the one case, or adding to it in the other, and thus restoring the equilibrium between its different kinds of produce. But these consequences, which would incontestably follow from the doctrine, that the price of corn immediately and entirely regulates the prices of labour and of all other commodities, are so directly contrary to all experience, that the doctrine itself cannot possibly be true; and we may be assured, that, whatever influence the price of corn may have upon other commodities, it is neither so immediate nor so complete, as to make this kind of produce an exception to all others.

That no such exception exists with regard to corn, is implied in all the general reasonings of the "Wealth of Nations." Dr. Smith evidently felt this; and wherever, in consequence, he does not shift the question from the exchangeable value of corn to its physical properties, he speaks with an unusual want of precision, and qualifies his positions by the expressions *much*, and in *any considerable degree*. But it should be recollected, that, *with* these qualifications, the argument is brought forward expressly for the purpose of shewing, that the rise of price, acknowledged to be occasioned by a bounty, on its first establishment, is nominal and not real.||Now, what is meant to be distinctly asserted here is, that a rise of price occasioned by a bounty upon the exportation or restrictions upon the importation of corn, cannot be less real than a rise of price to the same amount, occasioned by a course of bad seasons, an increase of population, the rapid progress of commercial wealth, or any other natural cause; and that, if Dr. Smith's argument, with its qualifications, be valid for the purpose for which it is advanced, it applies equally to an increased price occasioned by a natural demand.

Let us suppose, for instance, an increase in the demand and the price of corn, occasioned by an unusually prosperous state of our manufactures and foreign commerce; a fact which has frequently come within our own experience. According to the principles of supply and demand, and the general principles of the "Wealth of Nations," such an increase in the price of corn would give a decided stimulus to agriculture; and a more than usual quantity of capital would be laid out upon the land, as appears obviously to have been the case in this country during the last twenty years. According to the peculiar argument of Dr. Smith, however, no such stimulus could have been given to agriculture. The rise in the price of corn would have been immediately followed by a propor-||tionate rise in the price of labour and of all other commodities; and, though the farmer and landlord might have obtained, on an average, seventy-five shillings a quarter for their corn, instead of sixty, yet the farmer would not have been enabled to cultivate better, nor the landlord to live better. And thus it would appear, that agriculture is beyond the operation of that principle, which distributes the capital of a nation according to the varying profits of stock, in different employments; and that no increase of price can, at any time or in any country, materially accelerate the growth of corn, or determine a greater quantity of capital to agriculture.

The experience of every person, who sees what is going forward on the land, and the feelings and conduct both of farmers and landlords, abundantly contradict this reasoning.

Dr. Smith was evidently led into this train of argument, from his habit of considering labour as the standard measure of value, and corn as the measure of labour. But, that corn is a very inaccurate measure of labour, the history of our own country will amply demonstrate; where labour, compared with corn, will be found to have experienced very great and striking variations, not only from year to year, but from century to century; and for ten, twenty, and||thirty years together.[1] And that neither labour nor any other commodity can be an accurate measure of real value in exchange, is now considered as one of the most incontrovertible doctrines of political economy; and indeed follows, as a necessary consequence, from the very definition of value in exchange. But to allow that corn regulates the prices of all commodities, is at once to erect it into a standard measure of real value in exchange; and we must either deny the truth of Dr. Smith's argument, or acknowledge, that what seems to be quite impossible is found to exist; and that a given quantity of corn, notwithstanding the fluctuations to which its supply and demand must be subject, and the fluctuations to which the supply and demand of all the other commodities with which it is compared must also be subject, will, on the average of a few years, at all times and in all countries, purchase the same quantity of labour and of the necessaries and conveniences of life.

There are two obvious truths in political economy, which have not unfrequently been the sources of error.||

It is undoubtedly true, that corn might be just as successfully cultivated, and as much capital might be laid out upon the land, at the price of twenty shillings a quarter, as at the price of one hundred shillings, *provided* that every commodity, *both at home and abroad,* were precisely proportioned to the reduced

---

[1] From the reign of Edward III to the reign of Henry VII, a day's earnings, in corn, rose from a peck to near half a bushel; and from Henry VII to the end of Elizabeth, it fell from near half a bushel to little more than half a peck.

scale. In the same manner as it is strictly true, that the industry and capital of a nation would be exactly the same (with the slight exception at least of plate), if, in every exchange, both at home or abroad, one shilling only were used, where five are used now.

But to infer, from these truths, that any natural or artificial causes, which should raise or lower the values of corn or silver, might be considered as matters of indifference, would be an error of the most serious magnitude. Practically, no material change can take place in the value of either, without producing both lasting and temporary effects, which have a most powerful influence on the distribution of property, and on the demand and supply of particular commodities. The discovery of the mines of America, during the time that it raised the price of corn between three and four times, did not nearly so much as double the price of labour; and, while it permanently diminished the power of all fixed incomes, it gave a prodigious increase of power to all landlords and capitalists. In a similar manner,||the fall in the price of corn, from whatever cause it took place, which occurred towards the middle of the last century, accompanied as it was by a rise, rather than a fall in the price of labour, must have given a great relative check to the employment of capital upon the land, and a great relative stimulus to population; a state of things precisely calculated to produce the reaction afterwards experienced, and to convert us from an exporting to an importing nation.

It is by no means sufficient for Dr. Smith's argument, that the price of corn should determine the price of labour under precisely the same circumstances of supply and demand. To make it applicable to his purpose, he must shew, in addition, that a natural or artificial rise in the price of corn, or in the value of silver, will make no alteration in the state of property, and in the supply and demand of corn and labour; a position which experience uniformly contradicts.

Nothing then can be more evident both from theory and experience, than that the price of corn does not immediately and generally regulate the prices of labour and all other commodities; and that the real price of corn is capable of varying for periods of sufficient length to give a decided stimulus or discouragement to agriculture. It is, of course, only to a temporary encouragement||or discouragement, that any commodity, where the competition is free, can be subjected. We may increase the capital employed either upon the land or in the cotton manufacture, but it is impossible permanently to raise the profits of farmers or particular manufacturers above the level of other profits; and, after the influx of a certain quantity of capital, they will necessarily be equalized. Corn, in this respect, is subjected to the same laws as other commodities, and the difference between them is by no means so great as stated by Dr. Smith.

In discussing therefore the present question, we must lay aside the peculiar argument relating to the nature of corn; and allowing that it is possible to encourage cultivation by Corn Laws, we must direct our chief attention to the question of the policy or impolicy of such a system.

While our great commercial prosperity continues, it is scarcely possible that we should become again an exporting nation with regard to corn. The bounty has long been a dead letter, and will probably remain so. We may at present then confine our inquiry to the restrictions upon the importation of foreign corn with a view to an independent supply.

The determination of the question, respecting the policy or impolicy of continuing and||strengthening the Corn Laws, seems to depend upon the three following points:—

First, Whether, upon the supposition of the most perfect freedom of importation and exportation, it is probable that Great Britain and Ireland would grow an independent supply of corn.

Secondly, Whether an independent supply, if it do not come naturally, is an object really desirable, and one which justifies the interference of the legislature,

And, Thirdly, If an independent supply be considered as such an object, how far, and by what sacrifices, are restrictions upon importation adapted to attain the end in view.

Of the first point, it may be observed, that it cannot, in the nature of things, be determined by general principles, but must depend upon the size, soil, facilities of culture, and demand for corn in the country in question. We know that it answers to almost all small well peopled states, to import their corn; and there is every reason to suppose, that even a large landed nation, abounding in a manufacturing population, and having cultivated all its good soil, might find it cheaper to purchase a considerable part of its corn in other countries, where the supply, compared with the demand, was more abundant. If the intercourse between the different parts of||Europe were perfectly easy and perfectly free, it would be by no means natural that one country should be employing a great capital in the cultivation of poor lands, while at no great distance, lands comparatively rich were lying very ill cultivated, from the want of an effectual demand. The progress of agricultural improvement ought naturally to proceed more equably. It is true indeed that the accumulation of capital, skill, and population in particular districts, might give some facilities of culture not possessed by poorer nations; but such facilities could not be expected to make up for great differences in the quality of the soil and the expences of cultivation. And it is impossible to conceive that under very great inequalities in the demand for corn in different countries, occasioned by a very great difference in the accumulation of mercantile and manufacturing capital and in the number of large towns, an equalization of price could take place, without the transfer of a part of the general supply of Europe, from places where the demand was comparatively deficient, to those where it was comparatively excessive.

According to "Oddy's European Commerce," the Poles can afford to bring their corn to Dantzic at thirty-two shillings a quarter. The Baltic merchants are said to be of opinion that the price is not very different at present; and there||can be little doubt, that if the corn growers in the neighbourhood of the Baltic could look forward to a permanently open market in the British ports, they would raise corn expressly for the purpose. The same observation is applicable to America; and under such circumstances it would answer to both countries, for many years to come, to afford us supplies of corn, in much larger quantities than we have ever yet received from them.

During the five years from 1804 to 1808, both included, the bullion price of corn was about seventy-five shillings per quarter; yet, at this price, it answered to us better to import some portion of our supplies than to bring our land into such a state of cultivation as to grow our own consumption. We have already shewn how slowly and partially the price of corn affects the price of labour and some of the other expences of cultivation. Is it credible then that if by the freedom of importation the prices of corn were equalized, and reduced to about forty-five or fifty shillings a quarter, it could answer to us to go on improving our agriculture with our increasing population, or even to maintain our produce in its actual state?

It is a great mistake to suppose that the effects of a fall in the price of corn on cultivation may be fully compensated by a diminution of rents.||Rich land which yields a large neat rent, may indeed be kept up in its actual state, notwithstanding a fall in the price of its produce; as a diminution of rent may be made entirely to compensate this fall and all the additional expences that belong to a rich and highly-taxed country. But in poor land, the fund of rent will often be found quite insufficient for this purpose. There is a good deal of land in this country of such a quality that the expences of its cultivation, together with the outgoings of poor's rates, tithes and taxes, will not allow the farmer to pay more than a fifth or sixth of the value of the whole produce in the shape of rent. If we were to suppose the prices of grain to fall from seventy-five shillings to fifty shillings the quarter, the whole of such a rent would be absorbed, even if the price of the whole produce of the farm did not fall in proportion to the price of grain, and making some allowance for a fall in the price of labour. The regular cultivation of such land for grain would of course be given up, and any sort of pasture, however scanty, would be more beneficial both to the landlord and farmer.

But a diminution in the real price of corn is still more efficient, in preventing the future improvement of land, than in throwing land, which has been already improved, out of cultivation. In all progressive countries, the average price of corn is never higher than what is necessary to||continue the average increase of produce. And though, in much the greater part of the improved lands of most countries, there is what the French economists call a disposable produce, that is, a portion which might be taken away without interfering with future production, yet, in reference to the whole of the actual produce and the rate at which it is increasing, there is no part so disposable. In the employment of fresh capital upon the land to provide for the wants of an increasing population, whether this fresh capital be employed in bringing more land under the plough or in improving land already in cultivation, the main question always depends upon the expected returns of this capital; and no part of the gross profits can be diminished without diminishing the motive to this mode of employing it. Every diminution of price not fully and immediately balanced by a proportionate fall in all the necessary expences of a farm, every tax on the land, every tax on farming stock, every tax on the necessaries of of farmers, will tell in the computation; and if, after all these outgoings are allowed for, the price of the produce will not leave a fair remuneration for the capital employed, according to the general rate of profits and a rent at least equal to the rent of the land in its former state, no sufficient motive can exist to undertake the projected improvement.

It was a fatal mistake in the system of the||economists to consider merely production and reproduction, and not the provision for an increasing population, to which their territorial tax would have raised the most formidable obstacles.

On the whole then considering the present accumulation of manufacturing population in this country, compared with any other in Europe, the expences attending inclosures, the price of labour and the weight of taxes, few things seem less probable, than that Great Britain should naturally grow an independent supply of corn; and nothing can be more certain, than that if the prices of wheat in Great Britain were reduced by free importation nearly to a level with those of America and the continent, and if our manufacturing prosperity were to continue increasing, it would answer to us to support a part of our present population on foreign corn, and nearly the whole probably of the increasing population, which we may naturally expect to take place in the course of the next twenty or twenty-five years.

The next question for consideration is, whether an independent supply, if it do not come naturally, is an object really desirable and one which justifies the interference of the legislature.

The general principles of political economy teach us to buy all our commodities where we can have them the cheapest; and perhaps there is no general rule in the whole compass of the||science to which fewer justifiable exceptions can be found in practice. In the simple view of present wealth, population, and power, three of the most natural and just objects of national ambition, I can hardly imagine an exception; as it is only by a strict adherence to this rule that the capital of a country can ever be made to yield its greatest amount of produce.

It is justly stated by Dr. Smith that by means of trade and manufactures a country may enjoy a much greater quantity of subsistence, and consequently may have a much greater population, than what its own lands could afford. If Holland, Venice, and Hamburgh had declined a dependence upon foreign countries for their support, they would always have remained perfectly inconsiderable states, and never could have risen to that pitch of wealth, power, and population, which distinguished the meridian of their career.

Although the price of corn affects but slowly the price of labour, and never regulates it wholly, yet it has unquestionably a powerful influence upon it. A most perfect freedom of intercourse between different nations in the article of corn, greatly contributes to an equalization of prices and a level in the value of the precious metals. And it must be allowed that a country which possesses any peculiar facilities for successful exertion in manufacturing industry, can never make a full||and complete use of its advantages; unless the price of its labour and other commodities be reduced to that level compared with other countries, which results from the most perfect freedom of the corn trade.

It has been sometimes urged as an argument in favour of the Corn Laws, that the great sums which the country has had to pay for foreign corn during the last twenty years must have been injurious to her resources, and might have been saved by the improvement of our agriculture at home. It might with just as much propriety be urged that we lose every year by our forty millions worth of imports, and that we should gain by diminishing these extravagant purchases. Such a doctrine cannot be maintained without giving up the first and most fundamental principles of all commercial intercourse. No purchase is ever made, either at home or abroad, unless that which is received is, in the estimate of the purchaser, of more value than that which is given; and we may rest quite assured, that we shall never buy corn or any other commodities abroad, if we cannot by so doing supply our wants in a more advantageous manner, and by a smaller quantity of capital, than if we had attempted to raise these commodities at home.

It may indeed occasionally happen that in an unfavourable season, our exchanges with foreign countries may be affected by the necessity of mak-||ing unusually large purchases of corn; but this is in itself an evil of the slightest consequence, which is soon rectified, and in ordinary times is not more likely to happen, if our average imports were two millions of quarters, than if, on an average, we grew our own consumption. The *unusual* demand is in this case the sole cause of the evil, and not the average amount imported. The habit on the part of foreigners of supplying this amount, would indeed rather facilitate than impede further supplies; and as all trade is ultimately a trade of barter, and the power of purchasing cannot be permanently extended without an extension of the power of selling, the foreign countries which supplied us with corn would evidently have their power of purchasing our commodities increased, and would thus contribute more effectually to our commercial and manufacturing prosperity.

It has further been intimated by the friends of the Corn Laws, that by growing our own consumption we shall keep the price of corn within moderate bounds and to a certain degree steady. But this also is an argument which is obviously not tenable; as in our actual situation, it is only by keeping the price of corn up, very considerably above the average of the rest of Europe, that we can possibly be made to grow our own consumption.

A bounty upon exportation in one country,||may be considered, in some degree, as a bounty upon production in Europe; and if the growing price of corn in the country where the bounty is granted be not higher than in others, such a premium might obviously after a time have some tendency to create a temporary abundance of corn and a consequent fall in its price. But restrictions upon importation cannot have the slightest tendency of this kind. Their whole effect is to stint the supply of the general market, and to raise, not to lower, the price of corn.

Nor is it in their nature permanently to secure what is of more consequence, steadiness of prices. During the period indeed, in which the country is obliged regularly to import some foreign grain, a high duty upon it is effectual in steadily keeping up the price of home corn, and giving a very decided stimulus to agriculture. But as soon as the average supply becomes equal to the average consumption, this steadiness ceases. A plentiful year will occasion a sudden fall; and from the average price of the home produce being so much higher than in the other markets of Europe, such a fall can be but little relieved by exportation. It must be allowed, that a free trade in corn would in all ordinary cases not only secure a cheaper, but a more steady, supply of grain.

To counterbalance these striking advantages||of a free trade in corn, what are the evils which are apprehended from it?

It is alleged, first, that security is of still more importance than wealth, and that a great country likely to excite the jealousy of others, if it becomes dependent for the support of any considerable portion of its people upon foreign corn, exposes itself to the risk of having its most essential supplies suddenly fail at the time of its greatest need. That such a risk is not very great will be readily allowed. It would be as much against the interest of those nations which raised the superabundant supply as against the one which wanted it, that the intercourse should at any time be interrupted; and a rich country, which could afford to pay high for its corn, would not be likely to starve, while there was any to be purchased in the market of the commercial world.

At the same time it should be observed that we have latterly seen the most striking instances in all quarters, of governments acting from passion rather than interest. And though the recurrence of such a state of things is hardly to be expected, yet it must be allowed that if any thing resembling it should take place in future, when, instead of very nearly growing our own consumption, we were indebted to foreign countries for the support of two millions of our|| people, the distresses which our manufacturers suffered in 1812 would be nothing compared with the wide wasting calamity which would be then experienced.

According to the returns made to Parliament in the course of the last session, the quantity of grain and flour exported in 1811 rather exceeded, than fell short of, what was imported; and in 1812, although the average price of wheat was one hundred and twenty-five shillings the quarter, the balance of the importations of grain and flour was only about one hundred thousand quarters. From 1805, partly from the operation of the Corn Laws passed in 1804, but much more from the difficulty and expence of importing corn in the actual state of Europe and America, the price of grain had risen so high and had given such a stimulus to our agriculture, that with the powerful assistance of Ireland, we had been rapidly approaching to the growth of an independent supply. Though the danger therefore may not be great of depending for a considerable portion of our subsistence upon foreign countries, yet it must be acknowledged that nothing like an experiment has yet been made of the distresses that might be produced, during a widely extended war, by the united operation, of a great difficulty in finding a market for our manufactures, accompanied by the absolute necessity of supplying our-||selves with a very large quantity of foreign corn.

2dly. It may be said, that an *excessive* proportion of manufacturing population does not seem favourable to national quiet and happiness. Independently of any difficulties respecting the import of corn, variations in the channels of manufacturing industry and in the facilities of obtaining a vent for its produce are perpetually recurring. Not only during the last four or five years, but during the whole course of the war, have the wages of manufacturing labour been subject to great fluctuations. Sometimes they have been excessively high, and at other times proportionately low; and even during a peace they must always remain subject to the fluctuations which arise from the caprices of taste and fashion, and the competition of other countries. These fluctuations naturally tend to generate discontent and tumult and the evils which accompany them; and if to this we add, that the situation and employment of a manufacturer and his family are even in their best state unfavourable to health and virtue, it cannot appear desirable that a very large proportion of the whole society should consist of manufacturing labourers. Wealth, population and power are, after all, only valuable, as they tend to improve, increase, and secure the mass of human virtue and happiness.||

Yet though the condition of the individual employed in common manufacturing labour is not by any means desirable, most of the effects of manufactures and commerce on the general state of society are in the highest degree beneficial. They infuse fresh life and activity into all classes of the state, afford opportunities for the inferior orders to rise by personal merit and exertion, and stimulate the higher orders to depend for distinction upon other grounds than mere rank and riches. They excite invention, encourage science and the useful arts, spread intelligence and spirit, inspire taste for conveniences and comforts among the labouring classes; and, above all, give a new and happier structure to society, by increasing the proportion of the middle classes, that body on which the liberty, public spirit, and good government of every country must mainly depend.

If we compare such a state of society with a state merely agricultural, the general superiority of the former is incontestable; but it does not follow that the manufacturing system may not be carried to excess, and that beyond a certain point the evils which accompany it may not increase further than its advantages. The question, as applicable to this country, is not whether a manufacturing state is to be preferred to one merely agricultural, but whether a country the most manufacturing of any ever recorded in||history, with an agriculture however as yet nearly keeping pace with it, would be improved in its happiness, by a great relative increase to its manufacturing population and relative check to its agricultural population.

Many of the questions both in morals and politics seem to be of the nature of the problems *de maximis and minimis* in Fluxions; in which there is always a point where a certain effect is the greatest, while on either side of this point it gradually diminishes.

With a view to the permanent happiness and security from great reverses of the lower classes of people in this country, I should have little hesitation in thinking it desirable that its agriculture should keep pace with its manufactures, even at the expence of retarding in some degree the growth of manufactures; but it is a different question, whether it is wise to break through a general rule, and interrupt the natural course of things, in order to produce and maintain such an equalization.

3dly. It may be urged, that though a comparatively low value of the precious metals, or a high nominal price of corn and labour, tends rather to check commerce and manufactures, yet its effects are permanently beneficial to those who live by the wages of labour.

If the labourers in two countries were to earn the same quantity of corn, yet in one of them the||nominal price of this corn were twenty-five per cent higher than in the other, the condition of the labourers where the price of corn was the highest, would be decidedly the best. In the purchase of all commodities purely foreign; in the purchase of those commodities, the raw materials of which are wholly or in part foreign, and therefore influenced in a great degree by foreign prices, and in the purchase of all home commodities which are taxes, and not taxed ad valorem, they would have an unquestionable advantage: and these articles altogether are not inconsiderable even in the expenditure of a cottager.

As one of the evils therefore attending the throwing open our ports, it may be stated, that if the stimulus to population, from the cheapness of grain, should in the course of twenty or twenty-five years reduce the earnings of the labourer to the same quantity of corn as at present, at the same price as in the rest of Europe, the condition of the lower classes of people in this country would be deteriorated. And if they should not be so reduced, it is quite clear that the encouragement to the growth of corn will not be fully restored, even after the lapse of so long a period.

4thly. It may be observed, that though it might by no means be advisable to *commence* an artificial system of regulations in the trade of||corn; yet if, by such a system already established and other concurring causes, the prices of corn and of many commodities had been raised above the level of the rest of Europe, it becomes a different question, whether it would be advisable to risk the effects of so great and sudden a fall in the price of corn, as would be the consequence of at once throwing open our ports. One of the cases in which, according to Dr. Smith, "it may be a matter of deliberation how far it is proper to restore the free importation of foreign goods after it has been for some time interrupted, is, when particular manufactures, by means of high duties and prohibitions upon all foreign goods which can come into competition with them, have been so far extended as to employ a great multitude of hands[2]."

That the production of corn is not exempted from the operation of this rule has already been shewn; and there can be no doubt that the interests of a large body of landholders and farmers, the former to a certain extent permanently, and the latter temporarily, would be deeply affected by such a change of policy. These persons too may further urge, with much appearance of justice, that in being made to suffer this injury, they would not be treated fairly and impartially.

By protecting duties, drawbacks and taxes on almost all foreign commodities, capital is pre-||vented from leaving those trades, the prices of the products of which have been increased by domestic taxation: while if the ports were thrown open to the free admission of foreign corn, agriculture would be exposed to the loss of capital, occasioned by the competition of foreigners, who not being burdened by the same weight of taxation, would possess the most obvious advantages in the contest with our home growers. It may fairly indeed be said, that to restore the freedom of the corn trade, under these circumstances, is not really to restore things to their natural level, but to depress the cultivation of the land below its natural proportion to other kinds of industry. And though, even in this case, it might still be a national advantage to purchase corn where it could be had the cheapest;

---

[2] Wealth of Nations, b. iv, c. 2, p. 202.

yet it must be allowed that the owners of property in land would not be treated with strict impartiality.

If under all the circumstances of the case, it should appear impolitic to check our agriculture; and so desirable to secure an independent supply of corn, as to justify the continued interference of the legislature for this purpose, the next question for our consideration is;

Thirdly, How far and by what sacrifices, restrictions upon the importation of foreign corn are calculated to attain the end in view.

With regard to the mere practicability of ef-||fecting an independent supply, it must certainly be allowed that foreign corn may be so prohibited as completely to secure this object. A country which determines never to import corn, except when the price indicates a scarcity, will unquestionably in average years supply its own wants. But a law passed with this view might be so framed as to effect its object rather by a diminution of the people than an increase of the corn: and even if constructed in the most judicious manner, it can never be made entirely free from objections of this kind.

The evils which must always belong to restrictions upon the importation of foreign corn, are the following:

1. A certain waste of the national resources, by the employment of a greater quantity of capital than is necessary for procuring the quantity of corn required.

2. A relative disadvantage in all foreign commercial transactions, occasioned by the high comparative prices of corn and labour, and the low value of silver,

as far as they affect exportable commodities.

3. Some check to population, occasioned by a check to that abundance of corn, and demand for manufacturing labourers, which would be the result of a perfect freedom of importation.

4. The necessity of constant revision and in-||terference, which belong to almost every artificial system.

It is true, that during the last twenty years we have witnessed a very great increase of population and of our exported commodities, under a high price of corn and labour; but this must have happened in spite of these high prices, not in consequence of them; and is to be attributed chiefly to the unusual success of our inventions for saving labour and the unusual monopoly of the commerce of Europe which has been thrown into our hands by the war. When these inventions spread, and Europe recovers in some degree her industry and capital, we may not find it so easy to support the competition. The more strongly the natural state of the country directs it to the purchase of foreign corn, the higher must be the protecting duty or the price of importation, in order to secure an independent supply; and the greater consequently will be the relative disadvantage which we shall suffer in our commerce with other countries. This drawback may, it is certain, ultimately be so great as to counterbalance the effects of our extraordinary skill, capital and machinery.

The whole, therefore, is evidently a question of contending advantages and disadvantages; and, as interests of the highest importance are concerned, the most deliberation is required in its decision.||

In which ever way it is settled, some sacrifices must be submitted to. Those who contend for the unrestrained admission of foreign corn, must not imagine that the cheapness it will occasion will be an unmixed good; and that it will give an additional stimulus to the commerce and population of the country, while it leaves the present state of agriculture and its future increase undisturbed. They must be prepared to see a sudden stop put to the progress of our cultivation, and even some diminution of its actual state; and they must be ready to encounter the as yet untried risk, of making a considerable proportion of our population dependent upon foreign supplies of grain, and of exposing them to those vicissitudes and changes in the channels of commerce to which manufacturing states are of necessity subject.

On the other hand, those who contend for a continuance and increase of restrictions upon importation, must not imagine that the present state of agriculture and its present rate of eminence can be maintained without injuring other branches of the national industry. It is certain that they will not only be injured, but that they will be injured rather more than agriculture is benefited; and that a determination at all events to keep up the prices of our corn might involve us in a system of regulations, which, in the new state of Europe that is expected, might not||only retard in some degree, as hitherto, the progress of our foreign commerce, but ultimately begin to diminish it; in which case our agriculture itself would soon suffer, in spite of all our efforts to prevent it.

If, on weighing fairly the good to be obtained and the sacrifices to be made for it, the legislature should determine to adhere to its present policy of restrictions, it should be observed, in reference to the mode of doing it, that the time chosen is by no means favourable for the adoption of such a system of regulations as will not need future alterations. The state of the currency must throw the most formidable obstacles in the way of all arrangements respecting the prices of importation.

If we return to cash payments, while bullion continues of its present value compared with corn, labour, and most other commodities; little alteration will be required in the existing corn laws. The bullion price of corn is now very considerably under sixty-three shillings, the price at which the high duty ceases according to the act of 1804.

If our currency continues at its present nominal value, it will be necessary to make very considerable alterations in the laws, or they will be a mere dead letter and become entirely inefficient in restraining the importation of foreign corn.||

If, on the other hand, we should return to our old standard, and at the same time the value of bullion should fall from the restoration of general confidence, and the ceasing of an extraordinary demand for bullion; an intermediate sort of alteration will be necessary, greater than in the case first mentioned, and less than in the second.

In this state of necessary uncertainty with regard to our currency, it would be extremely impolitic to come to any *final regulation*, founded on an average which would be essentially influenced by the nominal prices of the last five years.

To these considerations it may be added, that there are many reasons to expect a more than usual abundance of corn in Europe during the repose to which we may now look forward. Such an abundance[3] took place after the termination of the wars of Louis XIV, and seems still more probable now, if the late devastation of the human race and interruption to industry, should be succeeded by a peace of fifteen or twenty years.

The prospect of an abundance of this kind may to some perhaps appear to justify still greater||efforts to prevent the introduction of foreign corn; and to secure our agriculture from too sudden a shock, it may be necessary to give it some protection. But if, under such circumstances with regard to the price of corn in Europe, we were to endeavour to retain the prices of the last five years, it is scarcely possible to suppose that our foreign commerce would not in a short time begin to languish. The difference between ninety shillings a quarter, or seventy-five shillings, the bullion price of 1808, and thirty-two or forty shillings a quarter, which are said to be the prices of the best wheat in France, is almost too great for our capital and machinery to contend with. The wages of labour in this country, though they have not risen in proportion to the price of corn, have been beyond all doubt considerably influenced by it.

---

[3] The cheapness of corn, during the first half of the last century, was rather oddly mistaken by Dr. Smith for a rise in the value of silver. That it was owing to peculiar abundance was obvious, from all other commodities rising instead of falling.

If the whole of the difference in the expence of raising corn in this country and in the corn countries of Europe was occasioned by taxation, and the precise amount of that taxation as affecting corn, could be clearly ascertained; the simple and obvious way of restoring things to their natural level and enabling us to grow corn in the same proportion as in a state of perfect freedom, would be to lay precisely the same amount of tax on imported corn and grant the same amount in a bounty upon exportation. Dr. Smith observes, that when the necessities of a||state have obliged it to lay a tax upon a home commodity, a duty of equal amount upon the same kind of commodity when imported from abroad, only tends to restore the level of industry which had necessarily been disturbed by the tax.[4]

---

[4] There is always however a very great difference between a direct tax, and the cost occasioned by indirect taxation. In the case of a direct tax, the amount of duty to be placed upon the similar foreign commodity, is not only precisely known, but is absolutely necessary, to prevent the evasion of the tax. In the case of the cost occasioned by indirect taxation, the precise amount can never be ascertained, nor is the duty on the foreign commodity necessary to the levying of the tax. Neither the inclination, nor the power to pay taxes on particular commodities, will be diminished by purchasing other commodities at a cheaper market. A British subject will not be more able to evade the numerous taxes which fall upon him, nor will he be less able to pay them by purchasing foreign corn. Yet it is still true, that British cultivation may suffer, compared with other countries, by indirect taxation. The duties on the other necessaries of life, besides corn, must raise its growing price, and give an advantage to the foreigner in the competition. It follows therefore, as was before intimated, that the landlord may suffer, and suffer partially, from the want of protecting duties on foreign corn, although neither the revenue of the government, nor the general wealth of the nation, might be benefited by them.

But the fact is that the whole difference of price does not by any means arise solely from taxation. A part of it, and I should think, no inconsiderable part, is occasioned by the necessity of yearly cultivating and improving more poor land, to provide for the demands of an increasing||population; which land must of course require more labour and dressing, and expence of all kinds in its cultivation. The growing price of corn therefore, independently of all taxation, is probably higher than in the rest of Europe; and this circumstance not only increases the sacrifice that must be made for an independent supply, but enhances the difficulty of framing a legislative provision to secure it.

When the former very high duties upon the importation of foreign grain were imposed, accompanied by the grant of a bounty, the growing price of corn in this country was not higher than in the rest of Europe; and the stimulus given to agriculture by these laws aided by other favourable circumstances occasioned so redundant a growth, that the average price of corn was not affected by the prices of importation. Almost the only sacrifice made in this case was the small rise of price occasioned by the bounty on its first establishment, which, after it had operated as a stimulus to cultivation, terminated in a period of increased cheapness.

If we were to attempt to pursue the same system in a very different state of the country, by raising the importation prices and the bounty in proportion to the fall in the value of money, the effects of the measure might bear very little resemblance to those which took place before. Since 1740 Great Britain has added||nearly four millions and a half to her population, and with the addition of Ireland probably eight millions, a greater proportion I believe than in any other country in Europe; and from the structure of our society and the great increase of the middle classes, the demands for the products of pasture have probably been augmented in a still greater proportion. Under these circumstances it is scarcely conceivable that any effects could make us again export corn to the same comparative extent as in the middle of the last century. An increase of the bounty in proportion to the fall in the value of money, would certainly not be sufficient; and probably nothing could accomplish it but such an excessive premium upon exportation, as would at once stop the progress of the population and foreign commerce of the country, in order to let the produce of corn get before it.

In the present state of things then we must necessarily give up the idea of creating a large average surplus. And yet very high duties upon importation, operating alone, are peculiarly liable to occasion great fluctuations of price. It has been already stated, that after they have succeeded in producing an independent supply by steady high prices, an abundant crop which cannot be relieved by exportation, must occasion a very sudden fall.[5] Should this continue a sec-

---

[5] The sudden fall of the price of corn this year seems to be a case precisely in point. It should be recollected however that quantity always in some degree balances cheapness.

ond||or third year, it would unquestionably discourage cultivation, and the country would again become partially dependent. The necessity of importing foreign corn would of course again raise the price to the price of importation, and the same causes might make a similar fall and a subsequent rise recur; and thus prices would tend to vibrate between the high prices occasioned by the high duties on importation and the low prices occasioned by a glut which could not be relieved by exportation.

It is under these difficulties that the parliament is called upon to legislate. On account of the deliberation which the subject naturally requires, but more particularly on account of the present uncertain state of the currency, it would be desirable to delay any final regulation. Should it however be determined to proceed *immediately* to a revision of the present laws, in order to render them more efficacious, there would be some obvious advantages, both as a temporary and permanent measure, in giving to the restrictions the form of a constant duty upon foreign corn, not to act as a prohibition, but as a protecting, and at the same time, profitable tax. And with a view to prevent the great fall that might be occasioned by a glut, under the circumstances before adverted to, but not to create an average||surplus, the old bounty might be continued, and allowed to operate in the same way as the duty at all times, except in extreme cases.

These regulations would be extremely simple and obvious in their operations, would give greater certainty to the foreign grower, afford a profitable tax to the government, and would be less affected even by the expected improvement of the currency, than high importation prices founded upon any past average.[6]

THE END.

---

[6] Since sending the above to the press I have heard of the new resolutions that are to be proposed. The machinery seems to be a little complicated; but if it will work easily and well, they are greatly preferable to those which were suggested last year.

To the free exportation asked, no rational objection can of course be made, though its efficiency in the present state of things may be doubted. With regard to the duties, if any be imposed, there must always be a question of degree. The principal objection which I see to the scale at first talked of or that since proposed, is the difference of its operation in the actual state of the currency, and on its restoration to its former value. With an average price of corn in the actual state of the currency, there will be a moderate competition of foreign grain, rather however too little than too much; whereas with an average price on the restoration of the currency, foreign competition will be absolutely and entirely excluded, and the fluctuations of price before adverted to, will be almost unavoidable.

THE GROUNDS OF AN OPINION
ON THE POLICY OF RESTRICTING
THE IMPORTATION OF FOREIGN CORN

(1815)

THE

GROUNDS

OF AN

OPINION

ON THE

POLICY OF RESTRICTING THE IMPORTATION

OF

FOREIGN CORN;

INTENDED AS

An Appendix

TO

"OBSERVATIONS ON THE CORN LAWS."

BY

THE REV. T. R. MALTHUS,

Professor of History and Political Economy in the East India College,
Hertfordshire.

LONDON:

PRINTED FOR JOHN MURRAY, ALBEMARLE STREET;
AND J. JOHNSON AND CO. ST. PAUL'S CHURCH YARD.

1815.

GROUNDS,

&c.

THE professed object of the *Observations on the Corn Laws,* which I published in the spring of 1814, was to state with the strictest impartiality the advantages and disadvantages which, in the actual circumstances of our present situation, were likely to attend the measures under consideration, respecting the trade in corn.

A fair review of both sides of the question, without any attempt to conceal the peculiar evils, whether temporary or permanent, which might belong to each, appeared to me of use, not only to assist in forming an enlightened decision on the subject, but particularly to prepare the public for the specific consequences which were to be expected from that decision, on whatever side it might be made. Such a preparation, from some quarter or||other, seemed to be necessary, to prevent those just discontents which would naturally have arisen, if the measure adopted had been attended with results very different from those which had been promised by its advocates, or contemplated by the legislature.

With this object in view, it was neither necessary, nor desirable, that I should myself express a decided opinion on the subject. It would hardly, indeed, have been consistent with that character of impartiality, which I wished to give to my statements, and in which I have reason to believe I in some degree succeeded.[1]

These previous statements, however, having been given, and having, I hope, shewn that the decision, whenever it is made, must be a compromise of contending advantages and disadvantages, I have no objection now to state, (without the least reserve), and I can truly say, with the most complete freedom from all interested motives, the grounds of a deliberate, yet decided, opinion in favour of some restrictions on the importation of foreign corn.

This opinion has been formed, as I wished||the readers of the *Observations* to form their opinions, by looking fairly at the difficulties on both sides of the question; and without vainly expecting to attain unmixed results, determining on which side there is the greatest balance of good with the least alloy of evil. The grounds on which the opinion so formed rests, are partly those which were stated in the *Observations,* and partly, and indeed mainly, some facts which have occured during the last year, and which have given, as I think, a decisive weight to the side of restrictions.

These additional facts are—

1st, The evidence, which has been laid before Parliament, relating to the effects of the present prices of corn, together with the experience of the present year.

---

[1] Some of my friends were of different opinions as to the side, towards which my arguments most inclined. This I consider as a tolerably fair proof of impartiality.

2dly, The improved state of our exchanges, and the fall in the price of bullion. And

3dly, and mainly, the actual laws respecting the exportation of corn lately passed in France.

In the *Observations on the Corn Laws*, I endeavoured to shew that, according to the general principles of supply and demand, a considerable fall in the price of corn could not take place, without throwing much poor land out of cultivation, and effectually preventing, for a considerable time, all farther||improvements in agriculture, which have for their object an increase of produce.

The general principles, on which I calculated upon these consequences, have been fully confirmed by the evidence brought before the two houses of Parliament; and the effects of a considerable fall in the price of corn, and of the expected continuance of low prices, have shewn themselves in a very severe shock to the cultivation of the country and a great loss of agricultural capital.

Whatever may be said of the peculiar interests and natural partialities of those who were called upon to give evidence upon this occasion, it is impossible not to be convinced, by the whole body of it taken together, that, during the last twenty years, and particularly during the last seven, there has been a great increase of capital laid out upon the land, and a great consequent extension of cultivation and improvement; that the system of spirited improvement and *high farming,* as it is technically called, has been principally encouraged by the progressive rise of prices owing in a considerable degree, to the difficulties

thrown in the way of the importation of foreign corn
by the war; that the rapid accumulation of capital
on the land, which it had occasioned, had so in-
creased||our home-growth of corn, that, notwith-
standing a great increase of population, we had become
much less dependent upon foreign supplies for our
support; and that the land was still deficient in capital, and would admit of the employment of such an
addition to its present amount, as would be competent
to the full supply of a greatly increased population:
but that the fall of prices, which had lately taken
place, and the alarm of a still further fall, from continued importation, had not only checked all progress
of improvement, but had already occasioned a considerable loss of agricultural advances; and that a
continuation of low prices would, in spite of a diminution of rents, unquestionably destroy a great mass of
farming capital all over the country, and essentially
diminish its cultivation and produce.

It has been sometimes said, that the losses at present sustained by farmers are merely the natural and
necessary consequences of overtrading, and that they
must bear them as all other merchants do, who have
entered into unsuccessful speculations. But surely the
question is not, or at least ought not to be, about the
losses and profits of farmers, and the present condition
of landholders compared with the past. It may be
necessary,||perhaps, to make inquiries of this kind,
with a view to ulterior objects; but the real question
respects the great loss of national wealth, attributed
to a change in the spirit of our legislative enactments
relating to the admission of foreign corn.

We have certainly no right to accuse our farmers of rash speculation for employing so large a capital in agriculture. The peace, it must be allowed, was most unexpected; and if the war had continued, the actual quantity of capital applied to the land, might have been as necessary to save the country from extreme want in future, as it obviously was in 1812, when, with the price of corn at above six guineas a quarter, we could only import a little more than 100,000 quarters. If, from the very great extension of cultivation, during the four or five preceding years, we had not obtained a very great increase of average produce, the distresses of that year would have assumed a most serious aspect.

There is certainly no one cause which can affect mercantile concerns, at all comparable in the extent of its effects, to the cause now operating upon agricultural capital. Individual losses must have the same distressing consequences in both cases, and they are often more complete, and the fall is greater, in the shocks||of commerce. But I doubt, whether in the most extensive mercantile distress that ever took in this country, there was ever one-fourth of the property, or one-tenth of the number of individuals concerned, when compared with the effects of the present rapid fall of raw produce, combined with the very scanty crop of last year.[2]

---

[2] Mercantile losses are always comparatively partial; but the present losses, occasioned by the unusual combination of low prices, and scanty produce, must inflict a severe blow upon the whole mass of cultivators. There never, perhaps, was known a year more injurious to the interests of agriculture.

Individual losses of course become national, according as they affect a greater mass of the national capital, and a greater number of individuals; and I think it must be allowed further, that no loss, in proportion to its amount, affects the interest of the nation so deeply, and vitally, and is so difficult to recover, as the loss of agricultural capital and produce.

If it be the intention of the legislature fairly to look at the evils, as well as the good, which belongs to both sides of the question, it must be allowed, that the evidence laid before the two houses of Parliament, and still more particularly the experience of the last year, shew, that the immediate evils which are capable of being remedied by a system of restrictions, are of no inconsiderable magnitude.||

2. In the *Observations on the Corn Laws,* I have, as a reason for some delay in coming to a final regulation respecting the price at which foreign corn might be imported, the very uncertain state of the currency. I observed, that three different importation prices would be necessary, according as our currency should either rise to the then price of bullion, should continue at the same nominal value, or should take an intermediate position, founded on a fall in the value of bullion, owing to the discontinuance of an extraordinary demand for it, and a rise in the value of paper, owing to the prospect of a return to payments in specie. In the course of this last year, the state of our exchanges, and the fall in the price of bullion, shew pretty clearly, that the intermediate alteration which, I then contemplated, greater than in the case first mentioned, and less than in the second, is the one

which might be adopted with a fair prospect of permanence; and that we should not now proceed under the same uncertainty respecting the currency, which we should have done, if we had adopted a final regulation in the early part of last year.[3] This||intermediate alteration, however, supposes a rise in the value of paper on a return to cash payments, and some general fall of prices quite unconnected with any regulations respecting the corn trade.[4]

But, if some fall of prices must take place from this cause, and if such a fall can never take place without a considerable check to industry, and discouragement to the accumulation of capital, it certainly does not seem a well-chosen time for the legislature to occasion another fall still greater, by departing at once from a system||of restrictions which it had pursued with steadiness during the greatest part of the last century

---

[3] At the same time, I certainly now very much wish that some regulation had been adopted last year. It would have saved the nation a great loss of agricultural capital, which it will take some time to recover. But it was impossible to foresee such a year as the present—such a combination, as a very bad harvest, and very low prices.

[4] I have very little doubt that the value of paper in this country has already risen, notwithstanding the increased issues of the Bank. These increased issues I attribute chiefly to the great failures which have taken place among country banks, and the very great purchases which have been made for the continental markets; and, under these circumstances, increased issues might take place, accompanied even by a rise of value. But the currency has not yet recovered itself. The real exchange, during the last year, must have been greatly in our favour, although the nominal exchange is considerably against us. This shews, incontrovertibly, that our currency is still depreciated, in reference to the bullion currencies of the continent. A part, however, of this depreciation may still be owing to the value of bullion in Europe not having yet fallen to its former level.

and, after having given up for a short period, had adopted again as its final policy in its two last enactments respecting the trade in corn. Even if it be intended, finally, to throw open our ports, it might be wise to pass some temporary regulations, in order to prevent the very great shock which must take place, if the two causes here noticed, of the depreciation of commodities, be allowed to produce their full effect by contemporaneous action.

3. I stated, in the Observations on the Corn Laws, that the cheapness and steadiness in the price of corn, which were promised by the advocates of restrictions, were not attainable by the measures they proposed; that it was really impossible for us to grow at home a sufficiency for our own consumption, without keeping up the price of corn considerably above the average of the rest of Europe; and that, while this was the case, as we could never export to any advantage, we should always be liable to the variations of price, occasioned by the glut of a superabundant harvest; in short, that it must be allowed that *a free trade in corn* would, in all ordinary cases, not only secure a cheaper, but a more steady, supply of grain.

In expressing this distinct opinion on the||effects of a free trade in corn, I certainly meant to refer to a trade *really free.*—that is, a trade by which a nation would be entitled to its share of the produce of the commercial world, according to its means of purchasing, whether that produce were plentiful or scanty. In this sense I adhere strictly to the opinion I then gave; but, since that period, an event has occurred which has shewn, in the clearest manner, that it is entirely out of our power, even in time of peace, to obtain a free trade in corn, or an approximation towards it, whatever may be our wishes on the subject.

It has, perhaps, not been sufficiently attended to in general, when the advantages of a free trade in corn have been discussed, that the jealousies and fears of nations, respecting their means of subsistence, will very rarely allow of a free egress of corn, when it is in any degree scarce. Our own statutes, till the very last year, prove these fears with regard to ourselves; and regulations of the same tendency occasionally come in aid of popular clamour in almost all countries of Europe. But the laws respecting the exportation of corn, which have been passed in France during the last year, have brought this subject home to us in the most striking and impressive manner. Our nearest neighbour, possessed of the largest and finest||corn country in Europe, and who, owing to a more favourable climate and soil, a more stationary and comparatively less crowded population, and a lighter weight of taxation, can grow corn at less than half our prices, has enacted, that the exportation of corn shall be free till the price rises to about forty-nine shillings a quarter,[5] and that then it shall entirely cease.[6]

---

[5] Calculated at twenty-four livres the pound sterling.

[6] It has been supposed by some, that this law cannot, and will not be executed: but I own I see no grounds for such an opinion. It is difficult to execute prohibitions against the exportation of corn, when it is in great plenty, but not when it is scarce. For ten years before 1757, we had in this country, regularly exported on an average, above 400,000 quarters of wheat, and in that year there was at once an excess of importation. With regard to the alledged impotence of governments in this respect, it appears to me that facts shew their power rather than their

From the vicinity of France, and the cheapness of its corn in all years of common abundance, it is scarcely possible that our main||imports should not come from that quarter as long as our ports are open to receive them. In this first year of open trade, our imports have been such, as to shew, that though the corn of the Baltic cannot seriously depress our prices in an unfavourable season at home, the corn of France may make it fall below a growing price, under the pressure of one of the worst crops that has been known for a long series of years.

I have at present before me an extract from a Rouen paper, containing the prices of corn in fourteen different markets for the first week in October, the average of which appears to be about thirty-eight shillings a quarter,[7] and this was after disturbances had taken place both at Havre and Dieppe, on account of the quantity exported, and the rise of prices which it had occasioned.

It may be said, perhaps, that the last harvest of France has been a very favourable one, and affords no just criterion of its general prices. But, from all that

[7] The average is 16 francs, 21 centimes, the Hectolitre. The Hectolitre is about 1-20th less than 3 Winchester bushels, which makes the English quarter come to about 38 shillings.

weakness. To be convinced of this, it is only necessary to look at the diminished importations from America during the war, and particularly from the Baltic after Bonaparte's decrees. The imports from France and the Baltic in 1810, were by special licenses, granted for purposes of revenue. Such licenses shewed strength rather than weakness; and might have been refused, if a greater object than revenue had at that time presented itself.

I hear, prices have often been as low during the last ten years. And, an average not exceeding forty shillings‖a quarter may, I think, be conclusively inferred from the price at which exportation is by law to cease.

At a time when, according to Adam Smith, the growing price in this country was only twenty-eight shillings a quarter, and the average price, including years of scarcity, only thirty-three shillings, exportation was not prohibited till the price rose to forty-eight shillings. It was the intention of the English government, at that time, to encourage agriculture by giving a vent to its produce. We may presume that the same motive influenced the government of France in the late act respecting exportation. And it is fair therefore to conclude, that the price of wheat, in common years, is considerably less than the price at which exportation is to cease.

With these prices so near us, and with the consequent power of supplying ourselves with great comparative rapidity, which in the corn trade is a point of the greatest importance, there can be no doubt that, if our ports were open, our principal supplies of grain would come from France; and that, in all years of common plenty in that country, we should import more largely from it than from the Baltic. But from this quarter, which would then become our main and most habitual source of‖supply, all assistance would be at once cut off, in every season of only moderate scarcity; and we should have to look to other quarters, from which it is an established fact, that large sudden supplies cannot be obtained, not only for our usual imports, and the natural variations which belong to them, but for those which had been suddenly cut off from France, and which our habitually deficient growth had now rendered absolutely necessary.

To open our ports, under these circumstances, is not to obtain a free trade in corn; and, while I should say, without hesitation, that a free trade in corn was calculated to produce steadier prices than the system of restrictions with which it has been compared, I should, with as little hesitation say, that such a trade in corn, as has been described, would be subject to much more distressing and cruel variations, than the most determined system of prohibitions.

Such a species of commerce in grain shakes the foundations, and alters entirely the *data* on which the general principles of free trade are established. For what do these principles say? They say, and say most justly, that if every nation were to devote itself particularly to those kinds of industry and produce, to which its soil, climate, situation, capital, and||skill, were best suited; and were then *freely to exchange* these products with each other, it would be the most certain and efficacious mode, not only of advancing the wealth and prosperity of the whole body of the commercial republic with the quickest pace, but of giving to each individual nation of the body the full and perfect use of all its resources.

I am very far indeed from meaning to insinuate, that if we cannot have the most perfect freedom of trade, we should have none; or that a great nation must immediately alter its commercial policy, whenever any of the countries with which it deals passes laws inconsistent with the principles of freedom. But

I protest most entirely against the doctrine, that we are to pursue our general principles without ever looking to see if they are applicable to the case before us; and that in politics and political economy, we are to go straight forward, as we certainly ought to do in morals, without any reference to the conduct and proceedings of others.

There is no person in the least acquainted with political economy, but must be aware that the advantages resulting from the division of labour, as applicable to nations as well as individuals, depend solely and entirely on the||power of exchanging subsequently the products of labour. And no one can hesitate to allow, that it is completely in the power of others to prevent such exchanges, and to destroy entirely the advantages which would otherwise result from the application of individual or national industry, to peculiar and appropriate products.

Let us suppose, for instance, that the inhabitants of the Lowlands of Scotland were to say to the Highlanders, "We will exchange our corn for your cattle, whenever we have a superfluity; but if our crops in any degree fail, you must not expect to have a single grain:" would not the question respecting the policy of the present change, which is taking place in the Highlands, rest entirely upon different grounds? Would it not be perfectly senseless in the Highlanders to think only of those general principles which direct them to employ the soil in the way that is best suited to it? If supplies of corn could not be obtained with some degree of steadiness and certainty from other quarters, would it not be absolutely necessary for them to grow it themselves, however ill adapted to it might be their soil and climate?

The same may be said of all the pasture districts of Great Britain, compared with the||surrounding corn countries. If they could only obtain the super-fluities of their neighbours, and were entitled to no share of the produce when it was scarce, they could not certainly devote themselves with any degree of safety to their present occupations.

There is, on this account, a grand difference be-tween the freedom of the home trade in corn, and the freedom of the foreign trade. A government of tol-erable vigour can make the home trade in corn really free. It can secure to the pasture districts, or the towns that must be fed from a distance, their share of the general produce, whether plentiful or scarce. It can set them quite at rest about the power of exchanging the peculiar products of their own labour for the other products which are necessary to them, and can dis-pense, therefore, to all its subjects, the inestimable advantages of an unrestricted intercourse.

But it is not in the power of any single nation to secure the freedom of the foreign trade in corn. To accomplish this, the concurrence of many others is necessary; and this concurrence, the fears and jeal-ousies so universally prevalent about the means of subsistence, almost invariably prevent. There is hardly a nation in Europe which does not occasionally exercise the power of stopping entirely, or||heavily taxing, its exports of grain, if prohibitions do not form part of its general code of laws.

The question then before us is evidently a special,

not a general one. It is not a question between the advantages of a free trade, and a system of restrictions; but between a specific system of restrictions formed by ourselves for the purpose of rendering us, in average years, nearly independent of foreign supplies, and the specific system of restricted importations, which alone it is in our power to obtain under the existing laws of France, and in the actual state of the other countries of the continent.[8]

In looking, in the first place, at the resources of the country, with a view to an independent supply for an increasing population; and comparing subsequently the advantages of the two systems abovementioned, without overlooking their disadvantages, I have fully made up my mind as to the side on‖ which the balance lies; and am decidedly of opinion, that a system of restrictions so calculated as to keep us, in average years, nearly independent of foreign supplies of corn, will more effectually conduce to the wealth and prosperity of the country, and of by far the greatest mass of the inhabitants, than the opening of our ports for the free admission of foreign corn, in the actual state of Europe.

Of the resources of Great Britain and Ireland for the further growth of corn, by the further application of capital to the land, the evidence laid before parliament furnishes the most ample testimony. But it is

---

[8] It appears from the evidence, that the corn from the Baltic is often very heavily taxed, and that this tax is generally raised in proportion to our necessities. In a scarce year in this country we could never get any considerable quantity of corn from the Baltic, without paying an enormous price for it.

not necessary, for this purpose, to recur to evidence that may be considered as partial. All the most intelligent works which have been written on agricultural subjects of late years, agree in the same statements; and they are confirmed beyond a possibility of doubt, when we consider the extraordinary improvements, and prodigious increase of produce that have taken place latterly in some districts, which, in point of natural soil, are not superior to others that are still yielding the most scanty and miserable crops. Most of the light soils of the kingdom might, with adequate capital and skill, be made to equal the improved parts of Norfolk; and the vast tracts of clay lands that are yet in a||degraded state almost all over the kingdom, are susceptible of a degree of improvement, which it is by no means easy to fix, but which certainly offers a great prospective increase of produce. There is even a chance (but on this I will not insist) of a diminution in the real price of corn,[9] owing to the extension of those great improvements, and that great economy and good management of labour, of which we have such intelligent accounts from Scotland.[10] If these clay lands, by draining, and the plentiful application of

---

[9] By the real growing price of corn I mean the real quantity of labour and capital which has been employed to procure the last additions which have been made to the national produce. In every rich and improving country there is a natural and strong tendency to a constantly increasing price of raw produce, owing to the necessity of employing, progressively, land of an inferior quality. But this tendency may be partially counteracted by great improvements in cultivation, and economy of labour. See this subject treated in *An Inquiry into the Nature and Progress of Rent*, just published.

[10] Sir John Sinclair's Account of the Husbandry of Scotland: and the General Report of Scotland.

lime and other manures, could be so far meliorated in quality as to admit of being worked by two horses and a single man, instead of three or four horses with a man and a boy, what a vast saving of labour and ex-||pense would at once be effected, at the same time that the crops would be prodigiously increased! And such an improvement may rationally be expected, from what has really been accomplished in particular districts. In short, if merely the best modes of cultivation, now in use in some parts of Great Britain, were generally extended, and the whole country was brought to a level, in proportion to its natural advantages of soil and situation, by the further accumulation and more equable distribution of capital and skill; the quantity of additional produce would be immense, and would afford the means of subsistence to a very great increase of population.

In some countries possessed of a small territory, and consisting perhaps chiefly of one or two large cities, it never can be made a question, whether or not they should freely import foreign corn. They exist, in fact, by this importation; and being always, in point of population, inconsiderable, they may, in general, rely upon a pretty regular supply. But whether regular or not, they have no choice. Nature has clearly told them, that if they increase in wealth and power to any extent, it can only be by living upon the raw produce of other countries.

It is quite evident that the same alternative||is not presented to Great Britain and Ireland, and that the United Empire has ample means of increasing in wealth, population, and power, for a very long course of years, without being habitually dependent upon foreign supplies for the means of supporting its inhabitants.

As we have clearly, therefore, our choice between two systems, under either of which we may certainly look forwards to a progressive increase of population and power; it remains for us to consider in which way the greatest portion of wealth and happiness may be steadily secured to the largest mass of the people.

1. And first let us look to the labouring classes of society, as the foundation on which the whole fabric rests; and, from their numbers, unquestionably of the greatest weight, in any estimate of national happiness.

If I were convinced, that to open our ports, would be permanently to improve the condition of the labouring classes of society, I should consider the question as at once determined in favour of such a measure. But I own it appears to me, after the most deliberate attention to the subject, that it will be attended with effects very different from those of improvement. We are very apt to be deceived by names, and to be captivated with||the idea of cheapness, without reflecting that the term is merely relative, and that it is very possible for a people to be miserably poor, and some of them starving, in a country where the money price of corn is very low. Of this the histories of Europe and Asia will afford abundant instances.

In considering the condition of the lower classes of society, we must consider only the real exchangeable value of labour; that is, its power of commanding the necessaries, conveniences, and luxuries of life.

I stated in the *Observations,* and more at large in the *Inquiry into Rents,*[11] that under the same demand for labour, and the same consequent power of purchasing the means of subsistence, a high *money price* of corn would give the labourer a very great advantage in the purchase of the conveniences and luxuries of life. The effect of this high money price would not, of course, be so marked among the very poorest of the society, and those who had the largest families; because so very great a part of their earnings must be employed in absolute necessaries. But to all those above the very poorest, the advantage of wages resulting||from a price of eighty shillings a quarter for wheat, compared with fifty or sixty, would in the purchase of tea, sugar, cotton, linens, soap, candles, and many other articles, be such as to make their condition decidedly superior.

Nothing could counterbalance this, but a much greater demand for labour; and such an increased demand, in consequence of the opening of our ports, is at best problematical. The check to cultivation has been so sudden and decisive, as already to throw a great number of agricultural labourers out of employment;[12] and in Ireland this effect has taken place to such a degree, as to threaten the most distressing, and even alarming, consequences. The farmers, in some

---

[11] "Inquiry into the Nature and Progress of Rent, and the Principles by which it is regulated."

[12] I was not prepared to expect (as I intimated in the *Observations*) so sudden a fall in the price of labour as has already taken place. This fall has been occasioned, not so much by the low price of corn, as by the sudden stagnation of agricultural work, occasioned by a more sudden check to cultivation than I foresaw.

districts, have entirely lost the little capital they possessed; and, unable to continue in their farms, have deserted them, and left their labourers without the means of employment. In a country, the peculiar defects of which were already a de-||ficiency of capital, and a redundancy of population, such a check to the means of employing labour must be attended with no common distress. In Ireland, it is quite certain, that there are no mercantile capitals ready to take up those persons who are thus thrown out of work, and even in Great Britain the transfer will be slow and difficult.

Our commerce and manufactures, therefore, must increase very considerably before they can restore the demand for labour already lost; and a moderate increase beyond this will scarcely make up for the disadvantage of a low money price of wages.

These wages will finally be determined by the usual money price of corn, and the state of the demand for labour.

There is a difference between what may be called the usual price of corn and the average price, which has not been sufficiently attended to. Let us suppose the common price of corn, for four years out of five, to be about £2 a quarter, and during the fifth year to be £6. The average price of the five years will then be £2 16s.; but the usual price will still be about £2, and it is by this price, and not by the price of a year of scarcity, or even the average including it, that wages are generally regulated.||

If the ports were open, the usual price of corn would certainly fall, and probably the average price; but from what has before been said of the existing laws of France, and of the practice among the Baltic nations of raising the tax on their exported corn in proportion to the demand for it, there is every reason to believe, that the fluctuations of price would be much greater. Such would, at least, be my conclusion from theory; and, I think, it has been confirmed by the experience of the last hundred years. During this time, the period of our greatest importations, and of our greatest dependance upon foreign corn, was from 1792 to 1805 inclusive; and certainly in no fourteen years of the whole hundred were the fluctuations of price so great. In 1792 the price was 42s. a quarter; in 1796, 77s.; in 1801, 118s. a quarter; and, in 1803, 56s. Between the year 1792 and 1801 the rise was almost a triple, and in the short period from 1798 to 1803, it rose from 50 to 118s. and fell again to 56.[13]||

I would not insist upon this experience as absolutely conclusive, on account of the mixture of accident in all such appeals to facts; but it certainly tends to confirm the probability of those great fluctuations

---

[13] I am strongly disposed to believe, that it is owing to the unwillingness of governments to allow the free egress of their corn, when it is scarce, that nations are practically so little dependent upon each other for corn, as they are found to be. According to all general principles they ought to be more dependent. But the great fluctuations in the price of corn, occasioned by this unwillingness, tend to throw each country back again upon its internal resources. This was remarkably the case with us in 1800 and 1801, when the very high price, which we paid for foreign corn, gave a prodigious stimulus to our domestic agriculture. A large territorial country, that imports foreign corn, is exposed not unfrequently to the fluctuations which belong to this kind of variable dependence, without obtaining the cheapness that ought to accompany a trade in corn really free.

which, according to all general principles, I should expect from the temper and customs of nations, with regard to the egress of corn, when it is scarce; and particularly from the existing laws of that country, which, in all common years, will furnish us with a large proportion of our supplies.

To these causes of temporary fluctuations, during peace, should be added the more durable as well as temporary, fluctuations occasioned by war. Without reference to the danger of excessive scarcity from another combination against us, if we are merely driven||back at certain distant intervals upon our own resources, the experience of the present times will teach us not to estimate lightly the convulsion which attends the return, and the evils of such alternations of price.

In the *Observations*, I mentioned some causes of fluctuations which would attend the system of restrictions; but they are in my opinion inconsiderable, compared with those which have been just referred to.

On the labouring classes, therefore, the effects of opening our ports for the free importation of foreign corn, will be greatly to lower their wages, and to subject them to much greater fluctuations of price. And, in this state of things, it will require a much greater increase in the demand for labour, than there is any rational ground for expecting, to compensate to the labourer the advantages which he loses in the high money wages of labour, and the steadier and less fluctuating price of corn.

2. Of the next most important class of society, those who live upon the profits of stock, one half

probably are farmers, or immediately connected with farmers; and of the property of the other half, not above one-fourth is engaged in foreign trade.

Of the farmers it is needless to say any||thing. It cannot be doubted that they will suffer severely from the opening of the ports. Not that the profits of farming will not recover themselves, after a certain period, and be as great, or perhaps greater, than they were before; but this cannot take place till after a great loss of agricultural capital, or the removal of it into the channels of commerce and manufactures.

Of the commercial and manufacturing part of the society, only those who are directly engaged in foreign trade, will feel the benefit of the importing system. It is of course to be expected, that the foreign trade of the nation will increase considerably. If it do not, indeed, we shall have experienced a very severe loss, without any thing like a compensation for it. And if this increase merely equals the loss of produce sustained by agriculture, the quantity of other produce remaining the same, it is quite clear that the country cannot possibly gain by the exchange, at whatever price it may buy or sell. Wealth does not consist in the dearness or cheapness of the usual measure of value, but in the quantity of produce; and to increase effectively this quantity of produce, after the severe check sustained by agriculture, it is necessary that commerce should make a very powerful start.||

In the actual state of Europe and the prevailing jealousy of our manufactures, such a start seems quite doubtful; and it is by no means impossible that we shall be obliged to pay for our foreign corn, by im-

porting less of other commodities, as well as by exporting more of our manufactures.

It may be said, perhaps, that a fall in the price of
our corn and labour, affords the only chance to our
manufacturers of retaining possession of the foreign
markets; and that though the produce of the country
may not be increased by the fall in the price of corn,
such a fall is necessary to prevent a positive diminution of it. There is some weight undoubtedly in this
argument. But if we look at the probable effects of
returning peace to Europe, it is impossible to suppose
that, even with a considerable diminution in the price
of labour, we should not lose some markets on the
continent, for those manufactures in which we have
no peculiar advantage; while we have every reason
to believe that in others, where our colonies, our navigation, our long credits, our coals, and our mines come
in question, as well as our skill and capital, we shall
retain our trade in spite of high wages. Under these
circumstances, it seems peculiarly advisable to main-
tain unimpaired, if possible, the home||market, and
not to lose the demand occasioned by so much of the
rents of land, and of the profits and capital of farmers,
as must necessarily be destroyed by the check to our
home produce.

But in whatever way the country may be affected
by the change, we must suppose that those who are
immediately engaged in foreign trade will benefit by
it. As those, however, form but a very small portion
of the class of persons living on the profits of stock,
in point of number, and not probably above a seventh
or eighth in point of property, their interests cannot

be allowed to weigh against the interests of so very large a majority.

With regard to this great majority, it is impossible that they should not feel very widely and severely the diminution of their nominal capital by the fall of prices. We know the magic effect upon industry of a rise of prices. It has been noticed by Hume, and witnessed by every person who has attended to subjects of this kind. And the effects of a fall are proportionately depressing. Even the foreign trade will not escape its influence, though here it may be counterbalanced by a real increase of demand. But, in the internal trade, not only will the full effect of this dead-||ening weight be experienced, but there is reason to fear that it may be accompanied with an actual diminution of home demand. There may be the same or even a greater quantity of corn consumed in the country, but a smaller quantity of manufactures and colonial produce; and our foreign corn may be purchased in part by commodities which were before consumed at home. In this case, the whole of the internal trade must severely suffer, and the wealth and enjoyments of the country be decidedly diminished. The quantity of a country's exports is a very uncertain criterion of its wealth. The quantity of produce permanently consumed at home is, perhaps, the most certain criterion of wealth to which we can refer.

Already, in all the country towns, this diminution of demand has been felt in a very great degree; and the surrounding farmers, who chiefly support them, are quite unable to make their accustomed purchases. If the home produce of grain be considerably diminished by the opening of our ports, of which there can be no doubt, these effects in the agricultural countries must be permanent, though not to the same extent as at present. And even if the manufacturing towns should ultimately increase, in proportion to the losses of the country, of which there is great reason to doubt, the||transfer of wealth and population will be slow, painful, and unfavourable to happiness.

3. Of the class of landholders, it may be truly said, that though they do not so actively contribute to the production of wealth, as either of the classes just noticed, there is no class in society whose interests are more nearly and intimately connected with the prosperity of the state.

Some persons have been of opinion, and Adam Smith himself among others, that a rise or fall of the price of corn does not really affect the interests of the landholders; but both theory and experience prove the contrary; and shew, that, under all common circumstances, a fall of price must be attended with a diminution of produce, and that a diminution of produce, will naturally be attended with a diminution of rent.[14]

Of the effect, therefore, of opening the ports, in diminishing both the real and nominal rents of the landlords, there can be no doubt; and we must not imagine that the interest of a body of men, so circumstanced as the landlords, can materially suffer without affecting the interests of the state.||

It has been justly observed by Adam Smith, that

---

[14] See this subject treated in *An Inquiry into the Nature and Progress of Rents.*

"no equal quantity of productive labour employed in manufactures can ever occasion so great a re-production as in agriculture." If we suppose the rents of land taken throughout the kingdom to be one-fourth of the gross produce, it is evident, that to purchase the same value of raw produce by means of manufactures, would require one-third more capital. Every five thousand pounds laid out on the land, not only repays the usual profits of stock, but generates an additional value, which goes to the landlord. And this additional value is not a mere benefit to a particular individual, or set of individuals, but affords the most steady home demand for the manufactures of the country, the most effective fund for its financial support, and the largest disposeable force for its army and navy. It is true, that the last additions to the agricultural produce of an improving country are not attended with a large proportion of rent;[15] and it is precisely this circumstance that may make it answer to a rich country to import some of its corn, if it can be secure of obtaining an equable supply. But in all cases the importation of foreign corn must fail to answer nationally, if it is not so much||cheaper than the corn that can be grown at home, as to equal both the profits and the rent of the grain which it displaces.

If two capitals of ten thousand pounds each, be employed, one in manufactures, and the other in the improvement of the land, with the usual profits, and withdrawn in twenty years,—the one employed in manufactures will leave nothing behind it, while the

---

[15] *Inquiry into the Nature and Progress of Rent.*

one employed on the land will probably leave a rent of no inconsiderable value.

These considerations, which are not often attended to, if they do not affect the ordinary question of a free trade in corn, must at least be allowed to have weight, when the policy of such a trade is, from peculiarity of situation and circumstances, rendered doubtful.

4. We now come to a class of society, who will unquestionably be benefited by the opening of our ports. These are the stockholders, and those who live upon fixed salaries.[16] They are not only, however, small in number, compared with those who will be affected in a different manner; but their interests are not so|| closely interwoven with the welfare of the state, as the classes already considered, particularly the labouring classes, and the landlords.

In the *Observations*, I remarked, that it was "an error of the most serious magnitude to suppose that any natural or artificial causes, which should raise or lower the values of corn or silver, might be considered as matters of indifference; and that, practically, no material change could take place in the values of either, without producing both temporary and lasting effects, which have a most powerful influence on the distribution of property."

In fact, it is perfectly impossible to suppose that, in any change in the measure of value, which ever did, or ever can take place practically, all articles, both

---

[16] It is to this class of persons that I consider myself as chiefly belonging. Much the greatest part of my income is derived from a fixed salary and the interest of money in the funds.

foreign and domestic, and all incomes, from whatever source derived, should arrange themselves precisely in the same relative proportions as before. And if they do not, it is quite obvious, that such a change may occasion the most marked differences in the command possessed by individuals and classes of individuals over the produce and wealth of the country. Sometimes the changes of this kind that actually take place, are favourable to the industrious classes of society, and sometimes unfavourable.||

It can scarcely be doubted, that one of the main causes, which has enabled us hitherto to support, with almost undiminished resources, the prodigious weight of debt which has been accumulated during the last twenty years, is the continued depreciation of the measure in which it has been estimated, and the great stimulus to industry, and power of accumulation, which have been given to the industrious classes of society by the progressive rise of prices. As far as this was occasioned by excessive issues of paper, the stockholder was unjustly treated, and the industrious classes of society benefited unfairly at his expense. But, on the other hand, if the price of corn were now to fall to fifty shillings a quarter, and labour and other commodities nearly in proportion, there can be no doubt that the stockholder would be benefited unfairly at the expense of the industrious classes of society, and consequently at the expense of the wealth and prosperity of the whole country.

During the twenty years, beginning with 1794 and ending with 1813, the average price of British corn per quarter was about eighty-three shillings; during the ten years ending with 1813, ninety-two shillings; and during the last five years of the twenty, one hundred and eight shillings. In the course of these twenty years,||the Government borrowed near five hundred millions of real capital, for which on a rough average, exclusive of the sinking fund, it engaged to pay about five per cent. But if corn should fall to fifty shillings a quarter, and other commodities in proportion, instead of an interest of about five per cent. the government would really pay an interest of seven, eight, nine, and for the last two hundred millions, ten per cent.

To this extraordinary generosity towards the stockholders, I should be disposed to make no kind of objection, if it were not necessary to consider by whom it is to be paid; and a moment's reflection will shew us, that it can only be paid by the industrious classes of society and the landlords, that is, by all those whose nominal incomes will vary with the variations in the measure of value. The nominal revenues of this part of the society, compared with the average of the last five years, will be diminished one half; and out of this nominally reduced income, they will have to pay the same nominal amount of taxation.

The interest and charges of the national debt, including the sinking fund, are now little short of forty millions a year; and these forty millions, if we completely succeed in the reduction of the price of corn and labour, are to be paid in future from a revenue of about half||the nominal value of the national income in 1813.

If we consider, with what an increased weight the

taxes on tea, sugar, malt, leather, soap, candles, &c. &c. would in this case bear on the labouring classes of society, and what *proportion* of their incomes all the active, industrious middle orders of the state, as well as the higher orders, must pay in assessed taxes, and the various articles of the customs and excise, the pressure will appear to be absolutely intolerable. Nor would even the *ad valorem* taxes afford any real relief. The annual forty millions, must at all events be paid; and if some taxes fail, others must be imposed that will be more productive.

These are considerations sufficient to alarm even the stockholders themselves. Indeed, if the measure of value were really to fall, as we have supposed, there is great reason to fear that the country would be absolutely unable to continue the payment of the present interest of the national debt.

I certainly do not think, that by opening our ports to the freest admission of foreign corn, we shall lower the price to fifty shillings a quarter. I have already given my reasons for believing that the fluctuations which in the present state of Europe, a system of importa-||tion would bring with it, would be often producing dear years, and throwing us back again upon our internal resources. But still there is no doubt whatever, that a free influx of foreign grain would in all commonly favourable seasons very much lower its price.

Let us suppose it lowered to sixty shillings a quarter, which for periods of three or four years together is not improbable. The difference between a measure of value at 60 compared with 80, (the price at which jt is proposed to fix the importation), is 33⅓ per cent. This per centage upon 40 millions amounts to a very formidable sum. But let us suppose that corn does not effectually regulate the prices of other commodities; and, making allowances on this account, let us take only 25, or even 20 per cent. Twenty per cent. upon 40 millions amounts at once to 8 millions,—a sum which ought to go a considerable way towards a peace establishment; but which, in the present case, must go to pay the additional interest of the national debt, occasioned by the change in the measure of value. And even if the price of corn be kept up by restrictions to 80 shillings a quarter, it is certain that the whole of the loans made during the war just terminated, will on an average, be paid at an interest very much higher than||they were contracted for; which increased interest can, of course, only be furnished by the industrious classes of society.

I own it appears to me that the necessary effect of a change in the measure of value on the weight of a large national debt is alone sufficient to make the question fundamentally different from that of a simple question about a free or restricted trade; and, that to consider it merely in this light, and to draw our conclusions accordingly, is to expect the same results from premises which have essentially changed their nature.

From this review of the manner in which the different classes of society will be affected by the opening of our ports, I think it appears clearly, that very much the largest mass of the people, and particularly of the industrious orders of the state, will be more injured than benefited by the measure.

I have now stated the grounds on which it appears to me to be wise and politic, in the actual circumstances of the country, to restrain the free importation of foreign corn.

To put some stop to the progressive loss of agricultural capital, which is now taking place, and which it will be by no means easy to recover, it might be advisable to pass a *temporary* act of restriction, whatever may be||the intention of the legislature in future. But, certainly it is much to be wished that as soon as possible, consistently with due deliberation, the permanent policy intended to be adopted with regard to the trade in corn should be finally settled. Already, in the course of little more than a century, three distinct changes in this policy have taken place. The act of William, which gave the bounty, combined with the prohibitory act of Charles II. was founded obviously and strikingly upon the principle of encouraging exportation and discouraging importation; the spirit of the regulations adopted in 1773, and acted upon some time before, was nearly the reverse, and encouraged importation and discouraged exportation. Subsequently, as if alarmed at the dependence of the country upon foreign corn, and the fluctuations of price which it had occasioned, the legislature in a feeble act of 1791, and rather a more effective one in 1804, returned again to the policy of restrictions. And if the act of 1804 be left now unaltered, it may be fairly said that a fourth change has taken place; as it is quite certain that, to proceed consistently upon a restrictive system, fresh regulations become absolutely necessary to keep pace with the progressive fall in the value of currency.||

Such changes in the spirit of our legislative enactments are much to be deprecated; and with a view to a greater degree of steadiness in future, it is quite necessary that we should be so fully prepared for the consequences which belong to each system, as not to have our determinations shaken by them, when they occur.

If, upon mature deliberation, we determine to open our ports to the free admission of foreign grain, we must not be disturbed at the depressed state, and diminished produce of our home cultivation; we must not be disturbed at our becoming more and more dependent upon other nations for the main support of our population; we must not be disturbed at the greatly increased pressure of the national debt upon the national industry; and we must not be disturbed at the fluctuations of price, occasioned by the very variable supplies, which we shall necessarily receive from France, in the actual state of her laws, or by the difficulty and expense of procuring large, and sudden imports from the Baltic, when our wants are pressing. These consequences may all be distinctly foreseen. Upon all general principles, they belong to the opening of our ports, in the actual state and relations of this country to the other countries of Europe; and though they may be counter-||balanced, or more than counterbalanced, by other advantages, they cannot, in the nature of things, be avoided.

On the other hand, if, on mature deliberation, we

determine steadily to pursue a system of restrictions with regard to the trade in corn, we must not be disturbed at a progressive rise in the price of grain; we must not be disturbed at the necessity of altering, at certain intervals, our restrictive laws according to the state of the currency, and the value of the precious metals; we must not be disturbed at the progressive diminution of fixed incomes; and we must not be disturbed at the occasional loss or diminution of a continental market for some of our least peculiar manufactures, owing to the high price of our labour.[17] All these disadvantages may be distinctly foreseen. According to all general principles they strictly belong to the system adopted; and, though they may be counterbalanced, and more than counterbalanced, by other greater advan-||tages, they cannot, in the nature of things, be avoided, if we continue to increase in wealth and population.

Those who promise low prices upon the restrictive system, take an erroneous view of the causes which determine the prices of raw produce, and draw an incorrect inference from the experience of the first half of the last century. As I have stated in another place,[18] a nation which very greatly gets the start of its neighbours in riches, without any peculiar natural facilities for growing corn, must necessarily submit to one of these alternatives—either a very high com-

[17] It often happens that the high prices of a particular country may diminish the *quantity* of its exports without diminishing the *value of their amount* abroad; in which case its foreign trade is peculiarly advantageous, as it purchases the same amount of foreign commodities at a much less expense of labour and capital.

[18] Inquiry into the Nature and Progress of Rent.

parative price of grain, or a very great dependence upon other countries for it.

With regard to the specific mode of regulating the importation of corn, if the restrictive system be adopted, I am not sufficiently acquainted with the details of the subject to be able to speak with confidence. It seems to be generally agreed, that, in the actual state of things, a price of about eighty shillings a quarter[19] would prevent our cultivation from falling||back, and perhaps allow it to be progressive. But, in future, we should endeavour, if possible, to avoid all discussions about the necessity of *protecting* the British farmer, and securing to him a *fair living profit*. Such language may perhaps be allowable in a crisis like the present. But certainly the legislature has nothing to do with securing to any classes of its subjects a particular rate of profits in their different trades. This is not the province of a government; and it is unfortunate that any language should be used which may convey such an impression, and make people believe that their rulers ought to listen to the accounts of their gains and losses.

But a government may certainly see sufficient reasons for wishing to secure an independent supply of grain. This is a definite, and may be a desirable, object, of the same nature as the Navigation Act; and it is much to be wished, that this object, and not the interests of farmers and landlords, should be the

---

[19] This price seems to be pretty fairly consistent with the idea of getting rid of that part of our high prices which belongs to excessive issues of paper, and retaining only that part which belongs to great wealth, combined with a system of restrictions.

ostensible, as well as the real, end which we have in view, in all our inquiries and proceedings relating to the trade in corn.

I firmly believe that, in the actual state of Europe, and under the actual circumstances of our present situation, it is our wisest policy to grow our own average supply of corn; and,||in so doing, I feel persuaded that the country has ample resources for a great and continued increase of population, of power, of wealth, and of happiness.

THE END.

AN INQUIRY INTO THE NATURE
AND PROGRESS OF RENT

(1815)

AN

INQUIRY

INTO

THE NATURE AND PROGRESS

OF

RENT,

AND THE

PRINCIPLES BY WHICH IT IS REGULATED.

———————

BY

THE REV. T. R. MALTHUS,

*Professor of History and Political Economy in the East India College,
Hertfordshire.*

———————

LONDON:

PRINTED FOR JOHN MURRAY, ALBEMARLE STREET.

1815.

[*Three Shillings and Sixpence.*]

ADVERTISEMENT.

The following Tract contains the substance of some notes on Rent, which, with others on different subjects relating to political economy, I have collected in the course of my professional duties at the East India College. It has been my intention, at some time or other, to put them in a form for publication; and the very near connexion of the subject of the present inquiry, with the topics immediately under discussion, has induced me to hasten its appearance at the present moment. It is the duty of those who have any means of contributing to the public stock of knowledge, not only to do so, but to do it at the time when it is most likely to be useful. If the nature of the disquisition should appear to the reader hardly to suit the form of a pamphlet, my apology must be, that it was not originally intended for so ephemeral a shape.

RENT, &c.

THE rent of land is a portion of the national revenue, which has always been considered as of very high importance.

According to Adam Smith, it is one of the three original sources of wealth, on which the three great divisions of society are supported.

By the Economists it is so pre-eminently distinguished, that it is considered as exclusively entitled to the name of riches, and the sole fund which is capable of supporting the taxes of the state, and on which they ultimately fall.

And it has, perhaps, a particular claim to our attention at the present moment, on account of the discussions which are going on respecting the Corn Laws, and the effects of rent on the price of raw produce, and the progress of agricultural improvement.

The rent of land may be defined to be that portion of the value of the whole produce||which remains to the owner of the land, after all the outgoings belonging to its cultivation, of whatever kind, have been paid, including the profits of the capital employed, estimated according to the usual and ordinary rate of the profits of agricultural stock at the time being.

179

It sometimes happens, that from accidental and temporary circumstances, the farmer pays more, or less, than this; but this is the point towards which the actual rents paid are constantly gravitating, and which is therefore always referred to when the term is used in a general sense.

The immediate cause of rent is obviously the excess of price above the cost of production at which raw produce sells in the market.

The first object therefore which presents itself for inquiry, is the cause or causes of the high price of raw produce.

After very careful and repeated revisions of the subject, I do not find myself able to agree entirely in the view taken of it, either by Adam Smith, or the Economists; and still less, by some more modern writers.

Almost all these writers appear to me to consider rent as too nearly resembling in its nature, and the laws by which it is governed, the excess of price above the cost of production, which is the characteristic of a monopoly.||

Adam Smith, though in some parts of the eleventh chapter of his first book he contemplates rent quite in its true light,[1] and has interspersed through his work more just observations on the subject than any

---

[1] I cannot, however, agree with him in thinking that all land which yields food must necessarily yield rent. The land which is successively taken into cultivation in improving countries, may only pay profits and labour. A fair profit on the stock employed, including, of course, the payment of labour, will always be a sufficient inducement to cultivate.

other writer, has not explained the most essential cause of the high price of raw produce with sufficient distinctness, though he often touches on it; and by applying occasionally the term monopoly to the rent of land, without stopping to mark its more radical peculiarities, he leaves the reader without a definite impression of the real difference between the cause of the high price of the necessaries of life, and of monopolized commodities.

Some of the views which the Economists have taken of the nature of rent appear to me, in like manner, to be quite just; but they have mixed them with so much error, and have drawn such preposterous and contradictory conclusions from them, that what is true in|| their doctrines, has been obscured and lost in the mass of superincumbent error, and has in consequence produced little effect. Their great practical conclusion, namely, the propriety of taxing exclusively the neat rents of the landlords, evidently depends upon their considering these rents as completely disposeable, like that excess of price above the cost of production which distinguishes a common monopoly.

Mr. Say, in his valuable Treatise on Political Economy, in which he has explained with great clearness many points which have not been sufficiently developed by Adam Smith, has not treated the subject of rent in a manner entirely satisfactory. In speaking of the different natural agents which, as well as the land, co-operate with the labours of man, he observes: "Heureusement personne nà pu dire le vent et le soleil m'appartiennent, et le service qu'ils rendent doit m'etre payè."[2] And, though he acknowledges that, for obvious reasons, property in land is necessary, yet he evidently considers rent as almost exclusively owing|| to such appropriation, and to external demand.

In the excellent work of M. de Sismondi, *De la Richesse Commerciale*, he says in a note on the subject of rent: "Cette partie de la rente foncière est celle que les Economistes ont decorée du nom du *produit net* comme étant le seul fruit du travail qui ajoutât quelquechore a la richesse nationale. On pourroit au contraire soutenir contre eux, que c'est la seule partie du produit du travail, dont la valeur soit purement nominale, et n'ait rien de réelle: c'est en effet le resultat de l'augmentation de prix qu'obtient un vendeur en vèrtu de son privilege, sans que la chose vendue eu vaille rèellement d'avantage."[3]

The prevailing opinions among the more modern writers in our own country, have appeared to me to incline towards a similar view of the subject; and, not to multiply citations, I shall only add, that in a very respectable edition of the *Wealth of Nations*, lately published by Mr. Buchanan, of Edinburgh, the idea of monopoly is pushed still farther. And while former writers, though they considered rent as governed by the laws of monopoly, were still of opinion that this monopoly in the case of||land was necessary and useful, Mr. Buchanan sometimes speaks of it even as

---

[2] Vol. II. p. 124. Of this work a new and much improved edition has lately been published, which is highly worthy the attention of all those who take an interest in these subjects.

[3] Vol. I. p. 49.

prejudicial, and as depriving the consumer of what it gives to the landlord.

In treating of productive and unproductive labour in the last volume, he observes,[4] that, "The neat surplus by which the Economists estimate the utility of agriculture, plainly arises from the high price of its produce, which, however advantageous to the landlord who receives it, is surely no advantage to the consumer who pays it. Were the produce of agriculture to be sold for a lower price, the same neat surplus would not remain, after defraying the expenses of cultivation; but agriculture would be still equally productive to the general stock; and the only difference would be, that as the landlord was formerly enriched by the high price, at the expense of the community, the community would now profit by the low price at the expense of the landlord. The high price in which the rent or neat surplus originates, while it enriches the landlord who has the produce of agriculture to sell, diminishes in the same proportion the wealth of those who are its purchasers; and on this account it is quite inaccurate to consider the landlord's rent as a clear|| addition to the national wealth." In other parts of his work he uses the same, or even stronger language, and in a note on the subject of taxes, he speaks of the high price of the produce of land as advantageous to those who receive it, but proportionably *injurious* to those who pay it. "In this view," he adds, "it can form no general addition to the stock of the community, as the neat surplus in question is nothing more than a revenue transferred from one class to another, and from

---

[4] Vol. IV. p. 134.

the mere circumstance of its thus changing hands, it is clear that no fund can arise out of which to pay taxes. The revenue which pays for the produce of land exists already in the hands of those who purchase that produce; and, if the price of subsistence were lower, it would still remain in their hands, where it would be just as available for taxation, as when by a higher price it is transferred to the landed proprietor."[5]

That there are some circumstances connected with rent, which have an affinity to a natural monopoly, will be readily allowed. The extent of the earth itself is limited, and cannot be enlarged by human demand. And the inequality of soils occasions, even at an early‖ period of society, a comparative scarcity of the best lands; and so far is undoubtedly one of the causes of rent properly so called. On this account, perhaps, the term *partial monopoly* might be fairly applicable. But the scarcity of land, thus implied, is by no means alone sufficient to produce the effects observed. And a more accurate investigation of the subject will shew us how essentially different the high price of raw produce is, both in its nature and origin, and the laws by which it is governed, from the high price of a common monopoly.

The causes of the high price of raw produce may be stated to be three.

First, and mainly, That quality of the earth, by which it can be made to yield a greater portion of the necessaries of life than is required for the maintenance of the persons employed on the land.

---

[5] Vol. III. p. 212.

2dly, That quality peculiar to the necessaries of life of being able to create their own demand, or to raise up a number of demanders in proportion to the quantity of necessaries produced.

And, 3dly, The comparative scarcity of the most fertile land.

The qualities of the soil and of its products, here noticed as the primary causes of the high price of raw produce, are the gifts of||nature to man. They are quite unconnected with monopoly, and yet are so absolutely essential to the existence of rent, that without them, no degree of scarcity or monopoly could have occasioned that excess of the price of raw produce, above the cost of production, which shews itself in this form.

If, for instance, the soil of the earth had been such, that, however well directed might have been the industry of man, he could not have produced from it more than was barely sufficient to maintain those, whose labour and attention were necessary to its products; though, in this case, food and raw materials would have been evidently scarcer than at present, and the land might have been, in the same manner, monopolized by particular owners; yet it is quite clear, that neither rent, nor any essential surplus produce of the land in the form of high profits, could have existed.

It is equally clear, that if the necessaries of life—the most important products of land, had not the property of creating an increase of demand proportioned to their increased quantity, such increased quantity would occasion a fall in their exchangeable value. However abundant might be the produce of a country, its population might remain stationary. And this abundance, without a proportionate demand,||and with a very high corn-price of labour, which would naturally take place under these circumstances, might reduce the price of raw produce, like the price of manufactures, to the cost of production.

It has been sometimes argued, that it is mistaking the principle of population, to imagine, that the increase of food, or of raw produce alone, can occasion a proportionate increase of population. This is no doubt true; but it must be allowed, as has been justly observed by Adam Smith, that "when food is provided, it is comparatively easy to find the necessary clothing and lodging." And it should always be recollected, that land does not produce one commodity alone, but in addition to that most indispensable of all commodities—food, it produces also the materials for the other necessaries of life; and the labour required to work up these materials is of course never excluded from the consideration.[6]||

It is, therefore, strictly true, that land produces the necessaries of life,—produces food, materials, and labour,—produces the means by which, and by which alone, an increase of people may be brought into being,

---

[6] It is, however, certain, that if either these materials be wanting, or the skill and capital necessary to work them up be prevented from forming, owing to the insecurity of property, or any other cause, the cultivators will soon slacken in their exertions, and the motives to accumulate and to increase their produce, will greatly diminish. But in this case there will be a very slack demand for labour; and, whatever may be the nominal cheapness of provisions, the labourer will not really be able to command such a portion of the necessaries of life, including, of course, clothing, lodging, &c. as will occasion an increase of population.

and supported. In this respect it is fundamentally different from every other kind of machine known to man; and it is natural to suppose, that it should be attended with some peculiar effects.

If the cotton machinery, in this country, were to go on increasing at its present rate, or even much faster; but instead of producing one particular sort of substance which may be used for some parts of dress and furniture, &c. had the qualities of land, and could yield what, with the assistance of a little labour, economy, and skill, could furnish food, clothing, and lodging, in such proportions as to create an increase of population equal to the increased supply of these necessaries; the demand for the products of such improved machinery would continue in excess above the cost of production, and this excess would no||longer exclusively belong to the machinery of the land.[7]

There is a radical difference in the cause of a demand for those objects which are strictly necessary to the support of human life, and a demand for all other commodities. In all other commodities the demand is exterior to, and independent of, the production itself; and in the case of a monopoly, whether natural or artificial, the excess of price is in proportion to the smallness of the supply compared with the demand, while this demand is comparatively unlimited. In the case of strict necessaries, the existence and increase of the demand, or of the number of demanders, must depend upon the existence and increase of these neces-

---

[7] I have supposed some check to the supply of the cotton machinery in this case. If there was no check whatever, the effects would shew themselves in excessive profits and excessive wages, without an excess above the cost of production.

saries themselves; and the excess of their price above the cost of their production must depend upon, and is permanently limited by, the excess of their quantity above the quantity necessary to maintain the labour required to produce them; without which excess of quantity no demand could have existed,||according to the laws of nature, for more than was necessary to support the producers.

It has been stated, in the new edition of the *"Wealth of Nations,"* that the cause of the high price of raw produce is, that such price is required to proportion the consumption to the supply.[8] This is also true, but it affords no solution of the point in question. We still want to know why the consumption and supply are such as to make the price so greatly exceed the cost of production, and the main cause is evidently the *fertility* of the earth in producing the necessaries of life. Diminish this plenty, diminish the fertility of the soil, and the excess will diminish; diminish it still further, and it will disappear. The cause of the high price of the necessaries of life above the cost of production, is to be found in their abundance, rather than their scarcity; and is not only essentially different from the high price occasioned by artificial monopolies, but from the high price of those peculiar products of the earth, not connected with food, which may be called natural and necessary monopolies.

The produce of certain vineyards in France, which, from the peculiarity of their soil and||situation, exclusively yield wine of a certain flavour, is sold of course at a price very far exceeding the cost of production.

[8] Vol. iv. p. 35.

And this is owing to the greatness of the competition for such wine, compared with the scantiness of its supply; which confines the use of it to so small a number of persons, that they are able, and rather than go without it, willing, to give an excessively high price. But if the fertility of these lands were increased, so as very considerably to increase the produce, this produce might so fall in value as to diminish most essentially the excess of its price above the cost of production. While, on the other hand, if the vineyards were to become less productive, this excess might increase to almost any extent.

The obvious cause of these effects is, that in all monopolies, properly so called, whether natural or artificial, the demand is exterior to, and independent of, the production itself. The number of persons who might have a taste for scarce wines, and would be desirous of entering into a competition for the purchase of them, might increase almost indefinitely, while the produce itself was decreasing; and its price, therefore, would have no other limit than the numbers, powers, and caprices, of the competitors for it.||

In the production of the necessaries of life, on the contrary, the demand is dependent upon the produce itself; and the effects are, in consequence, widely different. In this case, it is physically impossible that the number of demanders should increase, while the quantity of produce diminishes, as the demanders only exist by means of this produce. The fertility of soil, and consequent abundance of produce from a certain quantity of land, which, in the former case, diminished the excess of price above the cost of production, is, in the present case, the specific cause of such excess; and the diminished fertility, which in the former case might increase the price to almost any excess above the cost of production, may be safely asserted to be the sole cause which could permanently maintain the necessaries of life at a price not exceeding the cost of production.

Is it, then, possible to consider the price of the necessaries of life as regulated upon the principle of a common monopoly? Is it possible, with M. de Sismondi, to regard rent as the sole produce of labour, which has a value purely nominal, and the mere result of that augmentation of price which a seller obtains in consequence of a peculiar privilege: or, with Mr. Buchanan, to consider it as no addition to the national wealth, but merely as a trans-||fer of value, advantageous only to the landlords, and proportionably *injurious* to the consumers?

Is it not, on the contrary, a clear indication of a most inestimable quality in the soil, which God has bestowed on man—the quality of being able to maintain more persons than are necessary to work it. Is it not a part, and we shall see further on that it is an absolutely necessary part, of that surplus produce from the land,[9] which has been justly stated to be the

---

[9] The more general surplus here alluded to is meant to include the profits of the farmer, as well as the rents of the landlord; and, therefore, includes the whole fund for the support of those who are not directly employed upon the land. Profits are, in reality, a surplus, as they are in no respect proportioned (as intimated by the Economists) to the wants and necessities of the owners of capital. But they take a different course in the progress of society from rents, and it is necessary, in general, to keep them quite separate.

source of all power and enjoyment; and without which, in fact, there would be no cities, no military or naval force, no arts, no learning, none of the finer manufactures, none of the conveniences and luxuries of foreign countries, and none of that cultivated and polished society, which not only elevates and dignifies individuals, but which extends its||beneficial influence through the whole mass of the people?

In the early periods of society, or more remarkably perhaps, when the knowledge and capital of an old society are employed upon fresh and fertile land, this surplus produce, this bountiful gift of Providence, shews itself chiefly in extraordinary high profits, and extraordinary high wages, and appears but little in the shape of rent. While fertile land is in abundance, and may be had by whoever asks for it, nobody of course will pay a rent to a landlord. But it is not consistent with the laws of nature, and the limits and quality of the earth, that this state of things should continue. Diversities of soil and situation must necessarily exist in all countries. All land cannot be the most fertile: all situations cannot be the nearest to navigable rivers and markets. But the accumulation of capital beyond the means of employing it on land of the greatest natural fertility, and the greatest advantage of situation, must necessarily lower profits; while the tendency of population to increase beyond the means of subsistence must, after a certain time, lower the wages of labour.

The expense of production will thus be diminished, but the value of the produce, that is, the quantity of labour, and of the other pro-||ducts of labour besides corn, which it can command, instead of diminishing, will be increased. There will be an increasing number of people demanding subsistence, and ready to offer their services in any way in which they can be useful. The exchangeable value of food will, therefore, be in excess above the cost of production, including in this cost the full profits of the stock employed upon the land, according to the actual rate of profits, at the time being. And this excess is rent.

Nor is it possible that these rents should permanently remain as parts of the profits of stock, or of the wages of labour. If such an accumulation were to take place, as decidedly to lower the general profits of stock, and, consequently, the expenses of cultivation, so as to make it answer to cultivate poorer land; the cultivators of the richer land, if they paid no rent, would cease to be mere farmers, or persons living upon the profits of agricultural stock. They would unite the characters of farmers and landlords,—a union by no means uncommon; but which does not alter, in any degree, the nature of rent, or its essential separation from profits. If the general profits of stock were 20 per cent. and particular portions of land would yield 30 per cent. on the capital employed, 10 per cent. of the 30||would obviously be rent, by whomsoever received.

It happens, indeed, sometimes, that from bad government, extravagant habits, and a faulty constitution of society, the accumulation of capital is stopped, while fertile land is in considerable plenty, in which case profits may continue permanently very high; but even in this case wages must necessarily fall, which by reducing the expenses of cultivation must occasion rents. There is nothing so absolutely unavoidable in the progress of society as the fall of wages, that is such a fall as, combined with the habits of the labouring classes, will regulate the progress of population according to the means of subsistence. And when, from the want of an increase of capital, the increase of produce is checked, and the means of subsistence come to a stand, the wages of labour must necessarily fall so low, as only just to maintain the existing population, and to prevent any increase.

We observe in consequence, that in all those countries, such as Poland, where, from the want of accumulation, the profits of stock remain very high, and the progress of cultivation either proceeds very slowly, or is entirely stopped, the wages of labour are extremely low. And this cheapness of labour, by di-||minishing the expenses of cultivation, as far as labour is concerned, counteracts the effects of the high profits of stock, and generally leaves a larger rent to the landlord than in those countries, such as America, where, by a rapid accumulation of stock, which can still find advantageous employment, and a great demand for labour, which is accompanied by an adequate increase of produce and population, profits cannot be low, and labour for some considerable time remains very high.

It may be laid down, therefore, as an incontrovertible truth, that as a nation reaches any considerable degree of wealth, and any considerable fullness of population, which of course cannot take place without a great fall both in the profits of stock and the wages of labour, the separation of rents, as a kind of fixture upon lands of a certain quality, is a law as invariable as the action of the principle of gravity. And that rents are neither a mere nominal value, nor a value unnecessarily and injuriously transferred from one set of people to another; but a most real and essential part of the whole value of the national property, and placed by the laws of nature where they are, on the land, by whomsoever possessed, whether the landlord, the crown, or the actual cultivator.

Rent then has been traced to the same com-||mon nature with that general surplus from the land, which is the result of certain qualities of the soil and its products; and it has been found to commence its separation from profits, as soon as profits and wages fall, owing to the comparative scarcity of fertile land in the natural progress of a country towards wealth and population.

Having examined the nature and origin of rent, it remains for us to consider the laws by which it is governed, and by which its increase or decrease is regulated.

When capital has accumulated, and labour fallen on the most eligible lands of a country, other lands less favourably circumstanced with respect to fertility or situation, may be occupied with advantage. The expenses of cultivation, including profits, having fallen, poorer land, or land more distant from markets, though yielding at first no rent, may fully repay these expenses, and fully answer to the cultivator. And again, when either the profits of stock or the wages of labour, or both, have still further fallen, land still poorer, or still less favourably situated, may be taken into cultivation. And, at every step, it is clear, that if the price of produce does not fall, the rents of land will rise. And the price of produce will not fall, as long as the industry and ingenuity of the labouring classes, assisted by the capitals of‖those not employed upon the land, can find something to give in exchange to the cultivators and landlords, which will stimulate them to continue undiminished their agricultural exertions, and maintain their increasing excess of produce.

In tracing more particularly the laws which govern the rise and fall of rents, the main causes which diminish the expenses of cultivation, or reduce the cost of the instruments of production, compared with the price of produce, require to be more specifically enumerated. The principal of these seem to be four:— 1st, Such an accumulation of capital as will lower the profits of stock; 2dly, such an increase of population as will lower the wages of labour; 3dly, such agricultural improvements, or such increase of exertions, as will diminish the number of labourers necessary to produce a given effect; and 4thly, such an increase in the price of agricultural produce, from increased demand, as without nominally lowering the expense of production, will increase the difference between this expense and the price of produce.

The operation of the three first causes in lowering the expenses of cultivation, compared with the price of produce, are quite obvious; the fourth requires a few further observations.‖

If a great and continued demand should arise among surrounding nations for the raw produce of a particular country, the price of this produce would of course rise considerably; and the expenses of cultivation, rising only slowly and gradually to the same proportion, the price of produce might for a long time keep so much a head, as to give a prodigious stimulus to improvement, and encourage the employment of much capital in bringing fresh land under cultivation, and rendering the old much more productive.

Nor would the effect be essentially different in a country which continued to feed its own people, if instead of a demand for its raw produce, there was the same increasing demand for its manufactures. These manufactures, if from such a demand the value of their amount in foreign countries was greatly to increase, would bring back a great increase of value in return, which increase of value could not fail to increase the value of the raw produce. The demand for agricultural as well as manufactured produce would be augmented; and a considerable stimulus, though not perhaps to the same extent as in the last case, would be given to every kind of improvement on the land.

A similar effect would be produced by the||introduction of new machinery, and a more judicious division of labour in manufactures. It almost always happens in this case, not only that the quantity of manufactures is very greatly increased, but that the value of the whole mass is augmented, from the great extension of the demand for them, occasioned by their cheapness. We see, in consequence, that in all rich manufacturing and commercial countries, the value of manufactured and commercial products bears a very high proportion to the raw products;[10] whereas, in comparatively poor countries, without much internal trade and foreign commerce, the value of their raw produce constitutes almost the whole of their wealth. If we suppose the wages of labour so to rise with the rise of produce, as to give the labourer the same command of the means of subsistence as before, yet if he is able to purchase a greater quantity of other necessaries and conveniencies, both foreign and do-||mestic, with the price of a given quantity of corn, he may be equally well fed, clothed, and lodged, and population may be equally encouraged, although the wages of labour may not rise so high in proportion as the price of produce.

And even when the price of labour does really rise in proportion to the price of produce, which is a very rare case, and can only happen when the demand for labour precedes, or is at least quite contemporary with the demand for produce; it is so impossible that all the other outgoings in which capital is expended, should rise precisely in the same proportion, and at the same time, such as compositions for tithes, parish rates, taxes, manure, and the fixed capital accumulated under the former low prices, that a period of some continuance can scarcely fail to occur, when the

---

[10] According to the calculations of Mr. Colquhoun, the value of our trade, foreign and domestic, and of our manufactures, exclusive of raw materials, is nearly equal to the gross value derived from the land. In no other large country probably is this the case.—Treatise on the Wealth, Power, and Resources of the British Empire. p. 96. The whole annual produce is estimated at about 430 millions, and the products of agriculture at about 216 millions.

difference between the price of produce and the cost of production is increased.

In some of these cases, the increase in the price of agricultural produce, compared with the cost of the instruments of production, appears from what has been said to be only temporary; and in these instances it will often give a considerable stimulus to cultivation, by an increase of agricultural profits, without shewing itself much in the shape of rent. It||hardly ever fails, however, to increase rent ultimately. The increased capital, which is employed in consequence of the opportunity of making great temporary profits, can seldom or ever be entirely removed from the land, at the expiration of the current leases; and, on the renewal of these leases, the landlord feels the benefit of it in the increase of his rents.

Whenever then, by the operation of the four causes above mentioned, the difference between the price of produce and the cost of the instruments of production increases, the rents of land will rise.

It is, however, not necessary that all these four causes should operate at the same time; it is only necessary that the difference here mentioned should increase. If, for instance, the price of produce were to rise, while the wages of labour, and the price of the other branches of capital did not rise in proportion, and at the same time improved modes of agriculture were coming into general use, it is evident that this difference might be increased, although the profits of agricultural stock were not only undiminished, but were to rise decidedly higher.

Of the great additional quantity of capital employed

upon the land in this country, during||the last twenty
years, by far the greater part is supposed to have been
generated on the soil, and not to have been brought
from commerce or manufactures. And it was unquestionably the high profits of agricultural stock, occasioned by improvements in the modes of agriculture,
and by the constant rise of prices, followed only slowly
by a proportionate rise in the different branches of
capital, that afforded the means of so rapid and so
advantageous an accumulation.

In this case cultivation has been extended, and
rents have risen, although one of the instruments of
production, capital, has been dearer.

In the same manner a fall of profits and improvements in agriculture, or even one of them separately,
might raise rents, notwithstanding a rise of wages.

It may be laid down then as a general truth, that
rents naturally rise as the difference between the price
of produce and the cost of the instruments of production increases.

It is further evident, that no fresh land can be taken
into cultivation till rents have risen, or would allow
of a rise upon what is already cultivated.

Land of an inferior quality requires a great quantity
of capital to make it yield a given||produce; and, if the
actual price of this produce be not such as fully to compensate the cost of production, including the existing
rate of profits, the land must remain uncultivated. It
matters not whether this compensation is effected by
an increase in the money price of raw produce, without
a proportionate increase in the money price of the instruments of production, or by a decrease in the price

of the instruments of production, without a proportionate decrease in the price of produce. What is absolutely necessary, is a greater *relative* cheapness of the
instruments of production, to make up for the quantity of them required to obtain a given produce from
poor land.

But whenever, by the operation of one or more of
the causes before mentioned, the instruments of production become cheaper, and the difference between
the price of produce and the expenses of cultivation
increases, rents naturally rise. It follows therefore as a
direct and necessary consequence, that it can never
answer to take fresh land of a poorer quality into cultivation, till rents have risen or would allow of a rise,
on what is already cultivated.

It is equally true, that without the same tendency to
a rise of rents, occasioned by the operation of the same
causes, it cannot answer||to lay out fresh capital in the
improvement of old land,—at least upon the supposition, that each farm is already furnished with as
much capital as can be laid out to advantage, according to the actual rate of profits.

It is only necessary to state this proposition to make
its truth appear. It certainly may happen, and I fear
it happens frequently, that farmers are not provided
with all the capital which could be employed upon
their farms, at the actual rate of agricultural profits.
But supposing they are so provided, it implies distinctly, that more could not be applied without loss,
till, by the operation of one or more of the causes above
enumerated, rents had tended to rise.

It appears then, that the power of extending cultivation and increasing produce, both by the cultivation of fresh land and the improvement of the old, depends entirely upon the existence of such prices, compared with the expense of production, as would raise rents in the actual state of cultivation.

But though cultivation cannot be extended, and the produce of the country increased, but in such a state of things as would allow of a rise of rents, yet it is of importance to remark, that this rise of rents will be by no means in proportion to the extension of cultivation, or‖the increase of produce. Every relative fall in the price of the instruments of production, may allow of the employment of a considerable quanity of additional capital; and when either new land is taken into cultivation, or the old improved, the increase of produce may be considerable, though the increase of rents be trifling. We see, in consequence, that in the progress of a country towards a high state of cultivation, the quantity of capital employed upon the land, and the quantity of produce yielded by it, bears a constantly increasing proportion to the amount of rents, unless counterbalanced by extraordinary improvements in the modes of cultivation.[11]

---

[11] To the houour of Scotch cultivators, it should be observed, that they have applied their capitals so very skilfully and economically, that at the same time that they have prodigiously increased the produce, they have increased the landlord's proportion of it. The difference between the landlord's share of the produce in Scotland and in England is quite extraordinary— much greater than can be accounted for, either by the natural soil or the absence of tithes and poors rates.—See Sir John Sinclair's valuable Account of the Husbandry of Scotland; and the General Report not long since published—works replete with the most useful and interesting information on agricultural subjects.

According to the returns lately made to the Board of Agriculture, the average proportion which rent bears to the value of the whole||produce, seems not to exceed one fifth;[12] whereas formerly, when there was less capital employed, and less value produced, the proportion amounted to one fourth, one third, or even two fifths. Still, however, the numerical difference between the price of produce and the expenses of cultivation, increases with the progress of improvement; and though the landlord has a less *share* of the whole produce, yet this less share, from the very great increase of the produce, yields a larger quantity, and gives him a greater command of corn and labour. If the produce of land be represented by the number six, and the landlord has one-fourth of it, his share will be represented by one and a half. If the produce of land be as ten, and the landlord has one-fifth of it, his share will be represented by two. In the latter case, therefore, though the proportion of the landlord's share to the whole produce is greatly diminished, his real rent, independently of nominal price, will be increased in the proportion of from three to four. And in general, in all cases of increasing produce, if the landlord's share of this produce do not diminish in the same proportion, which though it often||happens during the currency of leases, rarely or never happens on the renewal of them, the real rents of land must rise.

We see then, that a progressive rise of rents seems to be necessarily connected with the progressive cultivation of new land, and the progressive improvement

---

[12] See Evidence before the House of Lords, given in by Arthur Young. p. 66.

of the old: and that this rise is the natural and necessary consequence of the operation of four causes, which are the most certain indications of increasing prosperity and wealth—namely, the accumulation of capital, the increase of population, improvements in agriculture, and the high price of raw produce, occasioned by the extension of our manufactures and commerce.

On the other hand, it will appear, that a fall of rents is as necessarily connected with the throwing of inferior land out of cultivation, and the continued deterioration of the land of a superior quality; and that it is the natural and necessary consequence of causes, which are the certain indications of poverty and decline, namely, diminished capital, diminished population, a bad system of cultivation, and the low price of raw produce.

If it be true, that cultivation cannot be extended but under such a state of prices, compared with the expenses of production, as will allow of an increase of rents, it follows natu-||rally that under such a state of relative prices as will occasion a fall of rents, cultivation must decline. If the instruments of production become dearer, compared with the price of produce, it is a certain sign that they are relatively scarce; and in all those cases where a large quantity of them is required, as in the cultivation of poor land, the means of procuring them will be deficient, and the land will be thrown out of employment.

It appeared, that in the progress of cultivation and of increasing rents, it was not necessary that all the instruments of production should fall in price at the same time; and that the difference between the price of produce and the expense of cultivation might increase, although either the profits of stock or the wages of labour might be higher, instead of lower.

In the same manner, when the produce of a country is declining, and rents are falling, it is not necessary that all the instruments of production should be dearer. In a declining or stationary country, one most important instrument of production is always cheap, namely, labour; but this cheapness of labour does not counterbalance the disadvantages arising from the dearness of capital; a bad system of culture; and, above all, a fall in the price of raw produce, greater than in the price of the other||branches of expenditure, which, in addition to labour, are necessary to cultivation.

It has appeared also, that in the progress of cultivation and of increasing rents, rent, though greater in positive amount, bears a less, and lesser proportion to the quantity of capital employed upon the land, and the quantity of produce derived from it. According to the same principle, when produce diminishes and rents fall, though the amount of rent will always be less, the proportion which it bears to capital and produce will always be greater. And, as in the former case, the diminished proportion of rent was owing to the necessity of yearly taking fresh land of an inferior quality into cultivation, and proceeding in the improvement of old land, when it would return only the common profits of stock, with little or no rent; so, in the latter case, the high proportion of rent is owing to the impossibility of obtaining produce, whenever a great expenditure is required, and the necessity of employing the reduced capital of the country, in the exclusive cultivation of its richest lands.

In proportion, therefore, as the relative state of prices is such as to occasion a progressive fall of rents, more and more lands will be gradually thrown out of cultivation, the remainder will be worse cultivated, and the diminution of||produce will proceed still faster than the diminution of rents.

If the doctrine here laid down, respecting the laws which govern the rise and fall of rents, be near the truth, the doctrine which maintains that, if the produce of agriculture were sold at such a price as to yield less neat surplus, agriculture would be equally productive to the general stock, must be very far from the truth.

With regard to my own conviction, indeed, I feel no sort of doubt that if, under the impression that the high price of raw produce, which occasions rent, is as injurious to the consumer as it is advantageous to the landlord, a rich and improved nation were determined by law, to lower the price of produce, till no surplus in the shape of rent any where remained; it would inevitably throw not only all the poor land, but all, except the very best land, out of cultivation, and probably reduce its produce and population to less than one-tenth of their former amount.

From the preceding account of the progress of rent, it follows, that the actual state of the natural rent of land is necessary to the actual produce; and that the price of produce, in every progressive country, must be just about equal to the cost of production on land of the||poorest quality actually in use; or to the cost of raising additional produce on old land, which yields only the usual returns of agricultural stock with little or no rent.

It is quite obvious that the price cannot be less; or such land would not be cultivated, nor such capital employed. Nor can it ever much exceed this price, because the poor land progressively taken into cultivation, yields at first little or no rent; and because it will always answer to any farmer who can command capital, to lay it out on his land, if the additional produce resulting from it will fully repay the profits of his stock, although it yields nothing to his landlord.

It follows then, that the price of raw produce, in reference to the *whole quantity* raised, is sold at the natural or necessary price, that is, at the price necessary to obtain the actual amount of produce, although by far the largest part is sold at a price very much above that which is necessary to its production, owing to this part being produced at less expense, while its exchangeable value remains undiminished.

The difference between the price of corn and the price of manufactures, with regard to natural or necessary price, is this; that if the price of any manufacture were essentially depressed, the whole manufacture would be|| entirely destroyed; whereas, if the price of corn were essentially depressed, the *quantity* of it only would be diminished. There would be some machinery in the country still capable of sending the commodity to market at the reduced price.

The earth has been sometimes compared to a vast machine, presented by nature to man for the produc-

tion of food and raw materials; but, to make the re-
semblance more just, as far as they admit of comparison, we should consider the soil as a present to man
of a great number of machines, all susceptible of continued improvement by the application of capital to
them, but yet of very different original qualities and
powers.

This great inequality in the powers of the machinery employed in procuring raw produce, forms one of
the most remarkable features which distinguishes the
machinery of the land from the machinery employed
in manufactures.

When a machine in manufactures is invented, which
will produce more finished work with less labour and
capital than before, if there be no patent, or as soon
as the patent is over, a sufficient number of such machines may be made to supply the whole demand, and
to supersede entirely the use of all the old ma-||chin-
ery. The natural consequence is, that the price is reduced to the price of production from the best machinery, and if the price were to be depressed lower, the
whole of the commodity would be withdrawn from the
market.

The machines which produce corn and raw materials on the contrary, are the gifts of nature, not the
works of man; and we find, by experience, that these
gifts have very different qualities and powers. The
most fertile lands of a country, those which, like the
best machinery in manufactures, yield the greatest
products with the least labour and capital, are never
found sufficient to supply the effective demand of an
increasing population. The price of raw produce,

therefore, naturally rises till it becomes sufficiently high to pay the cost of raising it with inferior machines, and by a more expensive process; and, as there cannot be two prices for corn of the same quality, all the other machines, the working of which requires less capital compared with the produce, must yield rents in proportion to their goodness.

Every extensive country may thus be considered as possessing a gradation of machines for the production of corn and raw materials, including in this gradation not only all the various qualities of poor land, of which every large territory has generally an abundance,||but the inferior machinery which may be said to be employed when good land is further and further forced for additional produce. As the price of raw produce continues to rise, these inferior machines are successively called into action; and, as the price of raw produce continues to fall, they are successively thrown out of action. The illustration here used serves to shew at once the necessity of the actual price of corn to the actual produce, and the different effect which would attend a great reduction in the price of any particular manufacture, and a great reduction in the price of raw produce.

I hope to be excused for dwelling a little, and presenting to the reader in various forms the doctrine, that corn in reference to the *quantity actually produced* is sold at its necessary price like manufactures, because I consider it as a truth of the highest importance, which has been entirely overlooked by the Economists, by Adam Smith, and all those writers who have represented raw produce as selling always at a monopoly price.

Adam Smith has very clearly explained in what manner the progress of wealth and improvement tends to raise the price of cattle, poultry, the materials of clothing and lodging, the most useful minerals, &c. &c. compared||with corn; but he has not entered into the explanation of the natural causes which tend to determine the price of corn. He has left the reader, indeed, to conclude, that he considers the price of corn as determined only by the state of the mines which at the time supply the circulating medium of the commercial world. But this is a cause obviously inadequate to account for the actual differences in the price of grain, observable in countries at no great distance from each other, and at nearly the same distance from the mines.

I entirely agree with him, that it is of great use to enquire into the causes of high price; as, from the result of such inquiry, it may turn out, that the very circumstance of which we complain, may be the necessary consequence and the most certain sign of increasing wealth and prosperity. But, of all inquiries of this kind, none surely can be so important, or so generally interesting, as an inquiry into the causes which affect the price of corn, and which occasion the differences in this price, so observable in different countries.

I have no hesitation in stating that, independently of irregularities in the currency of a country,[13] and

---

[13] In all our discussions we should endeavour, as well as we can, to separate that part of high price, which arises from excess of currency, from that part, which is natural, and arises from permanent causes. In the whole course of this argument, it is particularly necessary to do this.

other temporary and accidental||circumstances, the cause of the high comparative money price of corn is its high comparative real price, or the greater quantity of capital and labour which must be employed to produce it: and that the reason why the real price of corn is higher and continually rising in countries which are already rich, and still advancing in prosperity and population, is to be found in the necessity of resorting constantly to poorer land—to machines which require a greater expenditure to work them—and which consequently occasion each fresh addition to the raw produce of the country to be purchased at a greater cost— in short, it is to be found in the important truth that corn, in a *progressive country*, is sold at the price necessary to yield the actual supply; and that, as this supply becomes more and more difficult, the price rises in proportion.[14]||

The price of corn, as determined by these causes, will of course be greatly modified by other circumstances; by direct and indirect taxation; by improvements in the modes of cultivation; by the saving of labour on the land; and particularly by the importa-

---

[14] It will be observed, that I have said in a *progressive country*; that is, in a country which requires yearly the employment of a greater capital on the land, to support an increasing population. If there were no question about fresh capital, or an increase of people, and all the land were good, it would not then be true that corn must be sold at its necessary price. The actual price might be diminished; and if the rents of land were diminished in proportion, the cultivation might go on as before, and the same quantity be produced. It very rarely happens, however, that all the lands of a country actually occupied are good, and yield a good neat rent. And in all cases, a fall of prices must destroy agricultural capital during the currency of leases; and on their renewal there would not be the same power of production.

tions of foreign corn. The latter cause, indeed, may do away, in a considerable degree, the usual effects of great wealth on the price of corn; and this wealth will then shew itself in a different form.

Let us suppose seven or eight large countries not very distant from each other, and not very differently situated with regard to the mines. Let us suppose further, that neither their soils nor their skill in agriculture are essentially unlike; that their currencies are in a natural state; their taxes nothing; and that every trade is free, except the trade in corn.||Let us now suppose one of them very greatly to increase in capital and manufacturing skill above the rest, and to become in consequence much more rich and populous. I should say, that this great comparative increase of riches could not possibly take place, without a great comparative advance in the price of raw produce; and that such advance of price would, under the circumstances supposed, be the natural sign and absolutely necessary consequence, of the increased wealth and population of the country in question.

Let us now suppose the same countries to have the most perfect freedom of intercourse in corn, and the expenses of freight, &c. to be quite inconsiderable. And let us still suppose one of them to increase very greatly above the rest, in manufacturing capital and skill, in wealth and population. I should then say, that as the importation of corn would prevent any great difference in the price of raw produce, it would prevent any great difference in the quantity of capital laid out upon the land, and the quantity of corn obtained from it; that, consequently, the great increase of wealth could not take place without a great dependence on the other nations for corn; and that this dependence, under the circumstances supposed, would be the natural sign, and absolutely||necessary consequence of the increased wealth and population of the country in question.

These I consider as the two alternatives necessarily belonging to a great comparative increase of wealth; and the supposition here made will, with proper restrictions, apply to the state of Europe.

In Europe, the expenses attending the carriage of corn are often considerable. They form a natural barrier to importation; and even the country which habitually depends upon foreign corn, must have the price of its raw produce considerably higher than the general level. Practically, also, the prices of raw produce, in the different countries of Europe, will be variously modified by very different soils, very different degrees of taxation, and very different degrees of improvement in the science of agriculture. Heavy taxation, and a poor soil, may occasion a high comparative price of raw produce, or a considerable dependance on other countries, without great wealth and population; while great improvements in agriculture and a good soil may keep the price of produce low, and the country independent of foreign corn, in spite of considerable wealth. But the principles laid down are the general principles on the subject; and in applying them to any particular case, the particular circumstances of||such case must always be taken into the consideration.

With regard to improvements in agriculture, which

in similar soils is the great cause which retards the advance of price compared with the advance of produce; although they are sometimes very powerful, they are rarely found sufficient to balance the necessity of applying to poorer land, or inferior machines. In this respect, raw produce is essentially different from manufactures.

The real price of manufactures, the quantity of labour and capital necessary to produce a given quantity of them, is almost constantly diminishing; while the quantity of labour and capital, necessary to procure the last addition that has been made to the raw produce of a rich and advancing country, is almost constantly increasing. We see in consequence, that in spite of continued improvements in agriculture, the money price of corn is *cæteris paribus* the highest in the richest countries, while in spite of this high price of corn, and consequent high price of labour, the money price of manufactures still continues lower than in poorer countries.

I cannot then agree with Adam Smith, in thinking that the low value of gold and silver is no proof of the wealth and flourishing state||of the country, where it takes place. Nothing of course can be inferred from it, taken absolutely, except the abundance of the mines; but taken relatively, or in comparison with the state of other countries, much may be inferred from it. If we are to measure the value of the precious metals in different countries, and at different periods in the same country, by the price of corn and labour, which appears to me to be the nearest practical approximation that can be adopted (and in fact corn is the meas-

are used by Adam Smith himself), it appears to me to follow, that in countries which have a frequent commercial intercourse with each other, which are nearly at the same distance from the mines, and are not essentially different in soil; there is no more certain sign, or more necessary consequence of superiority of wealth, than the low value of the precious metals, or the high price of raw produce.[15]||

It is of importance to ascertain this point; that we may not complain of one of the most certain proofs of the prosperous condition of a country.

It is not of course meant to be asserted, that the high price of raw produce is, separately taken, advantageous to the consumer; but that it is the necessary concomitant of superior and increasing wealth, and that one of them cannot be had without the other.[16]

---

[15] This conclusion may appear to contradict the doctrine of the *level* of the precious metals. And so it does, if by *level* be meant level of value estimated in the usual way. I consider the doctrine, indeed, as quite unsupported by facts, and the comparisons of the precious metals to water perfectly inaccurate. The precious metals are always tending to a state of rest, or such a state of things as to make their movement unnecessary. But when this state of rest has been nearly attained, and the exchanges of all countries are nearly at par, the value of the precious metals in different countries, estimated in corn and labour, or the mass of commodities, is very far indeed from being the same. To be convinced of this, it is only necessary to look at England, France, Poland, Russia, and India, when the exchanges are at par. That Adam Smith, who proposes labour as the true measure of value at all times and in all places, could look around him, and yet say that the precious metals were always the highest in value in the richest countries, has always appeared to me most unlike his usual attention to found his theories on facts.

[16] Even upon the system of importation, in the actual state and situation of the countries of Europe, higher prices must accompany superior and increasing wealth.

With regard to the labouring classes of society, whose interests as consumers may be supposed to be most nearly concerned, it is a very shortsighted view of the subject, which contemplates, with alarm, the high price of corn as certainly injurious to them. The essentials to their well being are their own prudential ha-||bits, and the *increasing demand* for labour. And I do no scruple distinctly to affirm, that under similar habits, and a similar demand for labour, the high price of corn, when it has had time to produce its natural effects, so far from being a disadvantage to them, is a positive and unquestionable advantage. To supply the same demand for labour, the necessary price of production must be paid, and they must be able to command the same quantities of the necessaries of life, whether they are high or low in price.[17] But if

---

[17] We must not be so far deceived by the evidence before Parliament, relating to the want of connexion between the prices of corn and of labour, as to suppose that they are really independent of each other. The price of the necessaries of life, in fact, the cost of producing labour. The supply cannot proceed, if it be not paid; and though there will always be a little latitude, owing to some variations of industry and habits, and the distance of time between the encouragement to population and the period of the results appearing in the markets: yet it is a still greater error, to suppose the price of labour unconnected with the price of corn, than to suppose that the price of corn immediately and completely regulates it. Corn and labour rarely march quite abreast; but there is an obvious limit, beyond which they cannot be separated. With regard to the unusual exertions made by the labouring classes in periods of dearness, which produce the fall of wages noticed in the evidence, they are most meritorious in the individuals, and certainly favour the growth of capital. But no man of humanity could wish to see them constant and unremitted. They are most admirable as a temporary relief; but if they were constantly in action, effects of a similar kind would result from them, as from the population of a country being pushed to the

they are able to com-||mand the same quantity of necessaries, and receive a money price for their labour, proportioned to their advanced price, there is no doubt that, with regard to all the objects of convenience and comfort, which do not rise in proportion to corn, (and there are many such consumed by the poor) their condition will be most decidedly improved.

The reader will observe in what manner I have guarded the proposition. I am well aware, and indeed have myself stated in another place, that the price of provisions often rises, without a proportionate rise of labour: but this cannot possibly happen for any length of time, if the *demand for labour* continues increasing at the same rate, and the habits of the labourer are not altered, either with regard to||prudence, or the quantity of work which he is disposed to perform.

The peculiar evil to be apprehended is, that the high money price of labour may diminish the demand for it; and that it has this tendency will be readily allowed, particularly as it tends to increase the prices of exportable commodities. But repeated experience has shewn us that such tendencies are continually counter balanced, and more than counter balanced by other circumstances. And we have witnessed, in our own country, a greater and more rapid extension of

---

very extreme limits of its food. There would be no resources in a scarcity. I own I do not see, with pleasure, the great extension of the practice of task work. To work really hard during twelve or fourteen hours in the day, for any length of time, is too much for a human being. Some intervals of ease are necessary to health and happiness: and the occasional abuse of such intervals is no valid argument against their use.

foreign commerce, than perhaps was ever known, under the apparent disadvantage of a very great increase in the price of corn and labour, compared with the prices of surrounding countries.

On the other hand, instances every where abound of a very low money price of labour, totally failing to produce an increasing demand for it. And among the labouring classes of different countries, none certainly are so wretched as those, where the demand for labour, and the population are stationary, and yet the prices of provisions extremely low, compared with manufactures and foreign commodities. However low they may be, it is certain, that under such circumstances, no more will fall to the share of the labourer than is ne-|| cessary just to maintain the actual population; and his condition will be depressed, not only by the stationary demand for labour, but by the additional evil of being able to command but a small portion of manufactures or foreign commodities, with the little surplus which he may possess. If, for instance, under a stationary population, we suppose, that in average families two-thirds of the wages estimated in corn are spent in necessary provisions, it will make a great difference in the condition of the poor, whether the remaining one-third will command few or many conveniencies and comforts; and almost invariably, the higher is the price of corn, the more indulgences will a given surplus purchase.

The high or low price of provisions, therefore, in any country is evidently a most uncertain criterion of the state of the poor in that country. Their condition obviously depends upon other more powerful causes;

and it is probably true, that it is as frequently good, or perhaps more frequently so, in countries where corn is high, than where it is low.

At the same time it should be observed, that the high price of corn, occasioned by the difficulty of procuring it, may be considered as the ultimate check to the indefinite progress of a||country in wealth and population. And, although the actual progress of countries be subject to great variations in their rate of movement, both from external and internal causes, and it would be rash to say that a state which is well peopled and proceeding rather slowly at present, may not proceed rapidly forty years hence; yet it must be owned, that the chances of a future rapid progress are diminished by the high prices of corn and labour, compared with other countries.

It is, therefore, of great importance, that these prices should be increased as little as possible artificially, that is, by taxation. But every tax which falls upon agricultural capital tends to check the application of such capital, to the bringing of fresh land under cultivation, and the improvement of the old. It was shewn, in a former part of this inquiry, that before such application of capital could take place, the price of produce, compared with the instruments of production, must rise sufficiently to pay the farmer. But, if the increasing difficulties to be overcome are aggravated by taxation, it is necessary, that before the proposed improvements are undertaken, the price should rise sufficiently, not only to pay the farmer, but also the government. And every tax, which||falls on agricultural capital, either prevents a proposed improvement, or causes it to be purchased at a higher price.

When new leases are let, these taxes are generally thrown off upon the landlord. The farmer so makes his bargain, or ought so to make it, as to leave himself, after every expense has been paid, the average profits of agricultural stock in the actual circumstances of the country, whatever they may be, and in whatever manner they may have been affected by taxes, particularly by so general a one as the property tax. The farmer, therefore, by paying a less rent to his landlord on the renewal of his lease, is relieved from any peculiar pressure, and may go on in the common routine of cultivation with the common profits. But his encouragement to lay out fresh capital in improvements is by no means restored by his new bargain. This encouragement must depend, both with regard to the farmer and the landlord himself, exclusively on the price of produce, compared with the price of the instruments of production; and, if the price of these instruments have been raised by taxation, no diminution of rent can give relief. It is, in fact, a question, in which rent is not concerned. And, with a view to *progressive improvements,* it may be safely asserted, that the total||abolition of rents would be less effectual than the removal of taxes which fall upon agricultural capital.

I believe it to be the prevailing opinion, that the great expense of growing corn in this country is almost exclusively owing to the weight of taxation. Of the tendency of many of our taxes to increase the expenses of cultivation and the price of corn, I feel no doubt;

but the reader will see from the course of argument pursued in this inquiry, that I think a part of this price, and perhaps no inconsiderable part, arises from a cause which lies deeper, and is in fact the necessary result of the great superiority of our wealth and population, compared with the quality of our natural soil and the extent of our territory.

This is a cause which can only be essentially mitigated by the habitual importation of foreign corn, and a diminished cultivation of it at home. The policy of such a system has been discussed in another place; but, of course, every relief from taxation must tend, under any system, to make the price of corn less high, and importation less necessary.

In the progress of a country towards a high state of improvement, the positive wealth of the landlord ought, upon the principles which have been laid down, gradually to increase; although||his relative condition and influence in society will probably rather diminish, owing to the increasing number and wealth of those who live upon a still more important surplus[18]—the profits of stock.

The progressive fall, with few exceptions, in the value of the precious metals throughout Europe; the still greater fall, which has occurred in the richest countries, together with the increase of produce which has been obtained from the soil, must all conduce to make the landlord expect an increase of rents on the

---

[18] I have hinted before, in a note, that profits may, without impropriety, be called a surplus. But, whether surplus or not, they are the most important source of wealth, as they are, beyond all question, the main source of accumulation.

renewal of his leases. But, in re-letting his farms, he is liable to fall into two errors, which are almost equally prejudicial to his own interests, and to those of his country.

In the first place, he may be induced, by the immediate prospect of an exorbitant rent, offered by farmers bidding against each other, to let his land to a tenant without sufficient capital to cultivate it in the best way, and make the necessary improvements upon it. This is undoubtedly a most short-sighted policy, the bad effects of which have been strongly noticed|| by the most intelligent land surveyors in the evidence lately brought before Parliament; and have been particularly remarkable in Ireland, where the imprudence of the landlords in this respect, combined, perhaps, with some real difficulty of finding substantial tenants, has aggravated the discontents of the country, and thrown the most serious obstacles in the way of an improved system of cultivation. The consequence of this error is the certain loss of all that future source of rent to the landlord, and wealth to the country, which arises from increase of produce.

The second error to which the landlord is liable, is that of mistaking a mere temporary rise of prices, for a rise of sufficient duration to warrant an increase of rents. It frequently happens, that a scarcity of one or two years, or an unusual demand arising from any other cause, may raise the price of raw produce to a height, at which it cannot be maintained. And the farmers, who take land under the influence of such prices, will, in the return of a mere natural state of things, probably break, and leave their farms in a ruined and exhausted state. These short periods of high price are of great importance in generating capital upon the land, if the farmers are allowed to have the advantage of them; but, if they are||grasped at prematurely by the landlord, capital is destroyed, instead of being accumulated; and both the landlord and the country incur a loss, instead of gaining a benefit.

A similar caution is necessary in raising rents, even when the rise of prices seems as if it would be permanent. In the progress of prices and rents, rent ought always to be a little behind; not only to afford the means of ascertaining whether the rise be temporary or permanent, but even in the latter case, to give a little time for the accumulation of capital on the land, of which the landholder is sure to feel the full benefit in the end.

There is no just reason to believe, that if the lands were to give the whole of their rents to their tenants, corn would be more plentiful and cheaper. If the view of the subject, taken in the preceding inquiry, be correct, the last additions made to our home produce are sold at the cost of production, and the same quantity could not be produced from our own soil at a less price, even without rent. The effect of transferring all rents to tenants, would be merely the turning them into gentlemen, and tempting them to cultivate their farms under the superintendance of careless and uninterested bailiffs, instead of the vigilant eye of a master, who is deterred from carelessness by the fear||of ruin, and stimulated to exertion by the hope of a competence. The most numerous instances of successful industry, and well directed knowledge, have been found among those who have paid a fair rent for their lands; who have embarked the whole of their capital in their undertaking; and who feel it their duty to watch over it with unceasing care, and add to it whenever it is possible. But when this laudable spirit prevails among a tenantry, it is of the very utmost importance to the progress of riches, and the permanent increase of rents, that it should have the power as well as the will to accumulate; and an interval of advancing prices, not immediately followed by a proportionate rise of rents, furnishes the most effective powers of this kind. These intervals of advancing prices, when not succeeded by retrograde movements, most powerfully contribute to the progress of national wealth. And practically I should say, that when once a character of industry and economy has been established, temporary high profits are a more frequent and powerful source of accumulation, than either an increased spirit of saving, or any other cause that can be named.[19] It is the||only cause which seems capable of accounting for the prodigious accumulation among individuals, which must have taken place in this country during the last twenty years, and which has left us with a greatly increased capital, notwithstanding our vast annual destruction of stock, for so long a period.

Among the temporary causes of high price, which may sometimes mislead the landlord, it is necessary

---

[19] Adam Smith notices the bad effects of high profits on the habits of the capitalist. They may perhaps sometimes occasion extravagance; but generally, I should say, that extravagant habits were a more frequent cause of a scarcity of capital and high profits, than high profits of extravagant habits.

to notice irregularities in the currency. When they are likely to be of short duration, they must be treated by the landlord in the same manner as years of unusual demand. But when they continue so long as they have done in this country, it is impossible for the landlord to do otherwise than proportion his rent accordingly, and take the chance of being obliged to lessen it again, on the return of the currency to its natural state.

The present fall in the price of bullion, and the improved state of our exchanges, proves, in my opinion, that a much greater part of the difference between gold and paper was owing to commercial causes, and a peculiar demand||for bullion than was supposed by many persons; but they by no means prove that the issue of paper did not allow of a higher rise of prices than could be permanently maintained. Already a retrograde movement, not exclusively occasioned by the importations of corn, has been sensibly felt; and it must go somewhat further before we can return to payments in specie. Those who let their lands during the period of the greatest difference between notes and bullion, must probably lower them, whichever system may be adopted with regard to the trade in corn. These retrograde movements are always unfortunate; and high rents, partly occasioned by causes of this kind, greatly embarrass the regular march of prices, and confound the calculations both of the farmer and landlord.

With the cautions here noticed in letting farms, the landlord may fairly look forward to a gradual and permanent increase of rents; and, in general, not only to an increase proportioned to the rise in the *price* of produce, but to a still further increase, arising from an increase in the *quantity* of produce.

If in taking rents, which are equally fair for the landlord and tenant, it is found that in successive lettings they do not rise rather more than in proportion to the price of pro-||duce, it will generally be owing to heavy taxation.

Though it is by no means true, as stated by the Economists, that all taxes fall on the neat rents of the landlords, yet it is certainly true that they are more frequently taxed both indirectly as well as directly, and have less power of relieving themselves, than any other order of the state. And as they pay, as they certainly do, many of the taxes which fall on the capital of the farmer and the wages of the labourer, as well as those directly imposed on themselves; they must necessarily feel it in the diminution of that portion of the whole produce, which under other circumstances would have fallen to their share. But the degree in which the different classes of society are affected by taxes, is in itself a copious subject, belonging to the general principles of taxation, and deserves a separate inquiry.||

THE END.

STATEMENTS RESPECTING
THE EAST-INDIA COLLEGE
(SECOND EDITION, 1817)

STATEMENTS

RESPECTING THE

EAST-INDIA COLLEGE,

WITH AN

APPEAL TO FACTS,

IN

REFUTATION OF THE CHARGES

LATELY BROUGHT AGAINST IT,

IN THE

Court of Proprietors.

Second Edition with Alterations.

BY

THE REV. T. R. MALTHUS,

PROFESSOR OF HISTORY AND POLITICAL ECONOMY IN THE EAST-INDIA
COLLEGE, HERTFORDSHIRE, AND LATE FELLOW OF JESUS
COLLEGE, CAMBRIDGE.

LONDON:

1817.

PREFACE.

THE following statements, with the exception of the last head, were written some time since, on account of a rumour then prevailing of charges being meditated in the Court of Proprietors, which I thought were likely to be founded in an ignorance of the real state of the college;—of what it had done, and what it was doing, towards the accomplishment of the specific objects for which it was founded.

The silence of the Court of Proprietors on this subject, the quiet and good order of the college during the last year, and a great reluctance on my own part to appear before the public on such an occasion, without a very strong necessity, withheld me from publishing. But it is impossible to be silent, under the uncontradicted imputations brought forward in the Court of Proprietors, on the 18th of December, when I know them to be unfounded. I no longer hesitate, therefore, to send what I had written to the press, with the addition of a more specific refutation of the charges brought against the college, in the Court of Proprietors and elsewhere, at the present moment.

The reader will, I hope, excuse a few partial repetitions under the last head; as I think it probable that this part will be read by persons who may not have leisure or inclination to read the whole.||

I have put my name to the following statements, to show that I pledge my character to the truth of what I have asserted, according to the best of my knowledge and belief. It would be but fair, therefore, that those writers who may attempt to controvert them, and continue their attacks upon the college in the public prints, should adopt the same candid and manly mode of proceeding. If they do not, the inference will be pretty strong, that they cannot reveal their names without discovering to the public some probable motives for their attacks, different from a desire to promote the welfare and good government of India.

T. ROBERT MALTHUS.

January 4th, 1817.||

STATEMENTS,
&c.

THE disturbances which have occasionally taken place at the East-India college, together with the virulent attacks lately made upon it in the Court of Proprietors, have excited the attention of the public, and given rise to some very unfavorable opinions respecting its utility and efficiency. It has been even surmised that a petition might be presented to Parliament to withdraw that legislative sanction which was given to it at the time of the renewal of the East-India Company's Charter.

The abolition of an extensive establishment, the object of which is to give an improved education to those who are to be sent from this country to govern sixty millions of people in India, ought not, certainly, to be determined on without much consideration. Whatever measures may be dictated by the feelings of temporary disappointment and irritation experienced by some who are immediately connected with the institution, either as its patrons, or as parents and friends of those who are educated there, the great object that must be kept in view by the legislature and the public is, the good government of India. Unless it can be clearly made out, that the education necessary for the furtherance of this object can be given in some other and better way than in the college actually established, they will certainly hesitate, and be very sure of the ground on which they go, before they consent to its abolition, or withdraw from it that support and countenance which are necessary to preserve it from ultimately perishing. Every part of the subject, therefore, should be thoroughly well considered previously to the taking of any new step, either with a view to the suppression of the existing institution, and a return to the former system of casual education, or with a view to the formation of any new establishment, which may appear to promise a more successful accomplishment of the object. The whole subject may, perhaps, be advantageously resolved into the following questions;||and the answers to them are intended to furnish some materials for the determination of the important points to which they refer.

I. *What are the qualifications at present necessary for the civil service of the East-India Company, in the administration of their Indian territories?*

II. *Has any deficiency in those qualifications been actually experienced in such a degree as to be injurious to the service in India?*

III. *In order to secure the qualifications required for the service of the Company, is an appropriate establishment necessary?—and should it be of the nature of a school, or a college?*

IV. *Should such an establishment be in England or in India? or should there be an establishment in both countries?*

V. *Does it appear that the college actually established in Hertfordshire is upon a plan calculated to supply that part of the appropriate education of the civil servants of the Company which ought to be completed in Europe?*

VI. *Are the disturbances which have taken place in the East-India College to be attributed to any radical and necessary evils inherent in its constitution and discipline: or to adventitious and temporary causes, which are likely to be removed?*

VII. *Are the more general charges which have lately been brought against the college in the Court of Proprietors founded in truth? or are they capable of a distinct refutation, by an appeal to facts?*

SECTION I.

I. *What are the qualifications at present necessary for the civil service of the East-India Company, in the administration of their Indian territories?*

TO the first question, and parts of the others, it will be impossible to give an answer at once so able and so conclusive as by quoting largely from the *"Minute in Council"* of the Marquis Wellesley, dated August 18, 1800, containing the reasons which induced him to found a collegiate institution at Fort William.||

He begins with a masterly view of the gradual change which has taken place in the number, importance, and responsibility of the trusts confided to the civil servants of the Company, and the high qualifications necessary to fill them: after which he proceeds as follows:—

"The British possessions in India now constitute one of the most extensive and populous empires in the world. The immediate administration of the government of the various provinces and nations composing this empire is principally confided to European civil servants of the East-India Company. Those provinces, namely, Bengal, Behar, Orissa, and Benares; the Company's Jaghire in the Carnatic, the Northern Circars, the Baramhal, and other districts ceded by the peace of Seringapatam in 1792, which are under the more immediate and direct administration of the civil servants of the Company, are acknowledged to form the most opulent and flourishing part of India; in which property, life, civil order, and religious liberty, are more secure, and the people enjoy a larger

portion of the benefits of good government, than in
any other country in this quarter of the globe. The
duty and policy of the British government in India
require that the system of confiding the immediate
exercise of every branch and department of the civil
government to Europeans educated in its own service,
and subject to its own direct controul, should be dif-
fused as widely as possible; as well with a view to the
stability of our own interests, as to the happiness and
welfare of our native subjects. This principle formed
the basis of the wise and benevolent system introduced by Lord Cornwallis, for the improvement of
the internal government of the provinces immediately
subject to the presidency of Bengal.

"In proportion to the extension of this beneficial
system, the duties of the European civil servants of
the East-India Company are become of greater magnitude and importance. The denominations of *writer,*
factor and *merchant,* by which the several classes
of the civil service are still distinguished, are now
utterly inapplicable to the nature and extent of the
duties discharged and of the occupations pursued by
the civil servants of the Company.

"To dispense justice to millions of people of various
languages, manners, usages, and religions; to administer a vast and complicated system of revenue, through
districts equal in extent to some of the most considerable kingdoms in Europe; to maintain civil order in
one of the most populous and litigious regions in the
world; these are now the duties of the larger portion
of the civil servants of the Company. The senior merchants, composing the Courts of Circuit and Appeal

under the presidency of Bengal, exercise in each of these courts a jurisdiction of greater local extent,|| applicable to a larger population, and occupied in the determination of causes infinitely more intricate and numerous, than that of any regularly constituted courts of justice in any part of Europe. The senior or junior merchants employed in the several magistracies and Zillah courts, the writers or factors filling the stations of registrars and assistants to the several courts and magistrates, exercise, in different degrees, functions of a nature either purely judicial, or intimately connected with the administration of the police, and with the maintenance of the peace and good order of their respective districts. Commercial and mercantile knowledge is not only unnecessary throughout every branch of the judicial department; but those civil servants, who are invested with the powers of magistracy, or attached to the judicial department in any ministerial capacity, although bearing the denomination of merchants, factors, or writers, are bound by law, and by the solemn obligation of an oath, to abstain from every commercial and mercantile pursuit. The mercantile title which they bear not only affords no description of their duty, but is entirely at variance with it.

"The pleadings in the several courts, and all important judicial transactions, are conducted in the native languages. The law which the Company's judges are bound to administer throughout the country is not the law of England, but that law to which the natives had been long accustomed under their former sovereigns, tempered and mitigated by the voluminous regulations of the Governor General in Council, as well as by the general spirit of the British constitution.

"These observations are sufficient to prove, that no more arduous or complicated duties of magistracy exist in the world, *no qualifications more various or comprehensive can be imagined,* than those which are required from every British subject who enters the seat of judgment within the limits of the Company's empire in India.

"To the administration of revenue many of the preceding observations will apply with equal force. The merchants, factors, and writers, employed in this department, also, are bound to abjure the mercantile denomination appropriated to their respective classes in the Company's service; nor is it possible for a collector of the revenue, or for any civil servant employed under him, to discharge his duty with common justice either to the state or to the people, unless he shall be conversant in the language, manners, and usages of the country, and in the general principles of the law, as administered in their courts of justice. In addition to the ordinary judicial and executive functions of the judges, magistrates, and collectors, the judges and magistrates occasionally act in||the capacity of governors of their respective districts, employing military, and exercising other extensive powers. The judges, magistrates, and collectors, are also respectively required by law to propose, from time to time, to the Governor-General in Council, such amendments of the existing laws, or such new laws, as may appear to them to be necessary to the welfare and good government of their respective districts. In this view the civil

servants employed in the departments of judicature
and revenue constitute a species of subordinate legislative council to the Governor-General in Council,
and also a channel of communication by which the
government ought to be enabled, at all times, to ascertain the wants and wishes of the people. The remarks
applied to these two main branches of the civil service,
viz. those of Judicature and Revenue, are at least
equally forcible in their application to those branches
which may be described under the general terms of
political and financial departments, comprehending
the office of Chief Secretary, the various stations in the
Secretary's office, in the Treasury, and in the office of
Accountant-General; together with all public officers
employed in conducting the current business at the
seat of government. To these must be added the diplo-
matic branch, including the several residencies at the
courts of our dependent and tributary princes, or
other native powers of India.

"It is certainly desirable that all these stations
should be filled by the civil servants of the Company;
it is equally evident that qualifications are required
in each of these stations, either wholly foreign to commercial habits, or far exceeding the limits of a commercial education.

"Even that department of the empire, which is de-
nominated exclusively commercial, requires knowledge and habits different in a considerable degree
from those which form the mercantile character in
Europe. Nor can the Company's investment ever be
conducted with the greatest possible advantage and
honour to themselves, or with adequate justice to their

subjects, unless their commercial agents shall possess many of the qualifications of statesmen enumerated in the preceding observations. The manufacturers, and other industrious classes, whose productive labour is the source of the investment, bear so great a proportion to the total population of the Company's dominions, that the general happiness and prosperity of the country must essentially depend on the conduct of the commercial servants employed in providing the investment. Their conduct cannot be answerable to such a charge, unless they be conversant in the native languages, and in the customs and usages of the people, as well as in the laws by which the country is governed. The peace, order, and welfare of whole provinces, may be materially affected by the malversa-||tions, or even by the ignorance and errors of a commercial resident, whose management touches the dearest and most valuable interests, and enters into the domestic concerns of numerous bodies of people, active and acute from habitual industry, and jealous of any act of power injurious to their properties, or contrary to their prejudices and customs.

"The civil servants of the East-India Company, therefore, can no longer be considered as the agents of a *commercial concern:* they are, in fact, the ministers and officers of a *powerful sovereign:* they must now be viewed in that capacity with a reference not to their nominal, but to their real occupations. They are required to discharge the functions of magistrates, judges, ambassadors, and governors of provinces, in all the complicated and extensive relations of those sacred trusts and exalted stations, and under peculiar circumstances, which greatly enhance the solemnity of every public obligation, and the difficulty of every public charge. Their duties are those of statesmen in every other part of the world; with no other characteristic differences than the obstacles opposed by an unfavourable climate, a foreign language, the peculiar usages and laws of India, and the manners of its inhabitants."

Nothing can be added to these statements which can be expected to render them more clear, or to give them greater weight. They are quite decisive with regard to the qualifications required for the civil service of the East-India Company in India.

SECTION II.—*Has any deficiency in these qualifications been actually experienced in such a degree as to be injurious to the service in India?*

ON the second question, also, it will be most advantageous to hear the opinion of the Marquis Wellesley. He observes in the minute of August 18, 1800, "It may be useful in this place to review the course in which the junior civil servants of the East-India Company now enter upon the important duties of their respective stations; to consider to what degree they now possess or can attain any means of qualifying themselves sufficiently for those stations; and to examine whether the great body of the civil servants at any of the Presidencies can now be deemed competent to discharge their arduous and comprehensive trusts in a manner correspondent to the interests and honour of the British name in India, or to the prosperity and happiness of our native subjects.

"The age at which the writers usually arrive in India is from sixteen to eighteen. Their parents and friends in England, from a variety of considerations, are naturally desirous not only to‖accelerate the appointment at home, but to despatch the young men to India at the earliest possible period. Some of these young men have been educated with an express view to the civil service in India on principles utterly erroneous, and inapplicable to its actual condition. Conformably to this error, they have received a limited education, confined principally to commercial knowledge, and in no degree extended to those liberal studies which constitute the basis of education at public schools in England. Even this limited course of study is interrupted at the early period of fifteen or seventeen years.

"It would be superfluous to enter into any argument to demonstrate the absolute insufficiency of this class of young men to execute the duties of any station whatever in the civil service of the Company, beyond the menial, laborious, unwholesome duty of a mere copying-clerk. Those who have received the benefits of a better education have the misfortune to find the course of their studies prematurely interrupted at the critical period when its utility is first felt, and before they have been enabled to secure the fruits of early application.

"On the arrival of the writers in India, they are either stationed in the interior of the country, or employed in some office in the presidency. If stationed in the interior of the country, they are placed in situations which require a knowledge of the language and customs of the natives; or of the regulations and laws; or of the general principles of jurisprudence; or of the details of the established system of revenue; or of the nature of the Company's investment; or of many of these branches of information combined. In all these branches of knowledge the young writers are totally uninformed, and they are consequently totally unequal to their prescribed duties. In some cases their superior in office, experiencing no benefit from their services, leaves them unemployed. In this state many devote their time to those luxuries and enjoyments which their situation enables them to command, without making any effort to qualify themselves for the important stations to which they are destined. They remain sunk in indolence, until, from their station in the service, they succeed to offices of high public trust.

"Positive incapacity is the necessary result of these pernicious habits of inaction; the principles of public integrity are endangered, and the successful administration of the whole government exposed to hazard. This has been the unhappy course of many, who have conceived an early disgust in provincial stations against business to which they have found themselves unequal, and who have been abandoned to the effects of despondency and sloth."||

The Marquis goes on to say, that "even the young men whose dispositions are the most promising, if stationed in the interior of the country, at an early period after their arrival in India, labour under such disadvantages, that they can scarcely establish those foundations of useful knowledge indispensably necessary to enable them afterwards to execute the duties

of important stations with ability and credit. And
that, with regard to the young men attached to the
offices of the presidency, the most assiduous of them,
being occupied in the close and laborious application
to the hourly business of transcribing papers, are
seldom able to make advances in any other branch
of knowledge, and at the close of two or three years
they have generally lost the fruits of their European
studies, without having gained any useful knowledge
of Asiatic literature or business; while those, whose
dispositions lead them to idleness and dissipation,
finding greater temptations to indulgence and extravagance in the presidency than in the provinces, fall
into courses which destroy their health and fortunes;
and some of them succeeding in the ordinary progress
of the service to employments, their incapacity or
misconduct becomes conspicuous to the natives, dis-
graceful to themselves, and injurious to the State.

"Under all these early disadvantages," the Marquis
says, "it is highly creditable to the individual characters of the civil servants of the East-India Company, that so many instances have occurred in various
branches and departments of the civil service, at all
the presidencies, of persons who have discharged their
public duties with considerable respect and honour.

"It has been justly observed, that all the merits of
the civil servants are to be ascribed to their own character, talents, and exertions; while their defects must
be imputed to the constitution and practice of the
service, which have not been accommodated to the
progressive changes of our situation in India, and
have not kept pace with the growth of this empire,

or with the increasing extent and importance of the functions and duties of civil servants.

"The study and acquisition of the languages have, however, been extended in Bengal, and the general knowledge and qualifications of the civil servants have been improved. The proportion of the civil servants in Bengal who have made a considerable progress towards the attainment of the qualifications requisite in their several stations appears great, and even astonishing, when viewed with regard to the early disadvantages, embarrassments, and defects of the civil service. But this proportion will appear very different when compared with the exigencies of the state, with the magnitude of these provinces, and with the total number||of the civil servants which must supply the succession to the great offices of the government.

"It must be admitted that the great body of the civil servants in Bengal is not at present sufficiently qualified to discharge the duties of the several arduous stations in the administration of this empire; and that it is particularly deficient in the judicial, fiscal, financial, and political branches of the government.

"The state of the civil services of Madras and Bombay is still more defective than that of Bengal."

Nothing can be more clear and convincing than this statement of deficiency in the great body of the civil servants of the Company, before any efforts were made, either in India or in England, to give them a superior education. It is sufficiently well known, though no written documents may remain on the subject, on account of no specific remedy having been proposed, that Lord Cornwallis found the same difficulty in filling the important offices of the state with proper persons as the Marquis Wellesley. Many of the older civil servants were passed over in the search for the qualifications required, and, even with the greatest range that the rules of the service would admit, the search was not always successful.

Mr. Edmonstone, in his excellent speech at the public disputation, held at the College of Fort-William on the 27th of July, 1815, strongly notices the former defects in the education of the civil servants, and adverts particularly to the argument adduced by some persons in favor of the sufficiency of the old system, founded on the progressive prosperity and power of the British dominion in India, and on the success which attended the administration of the concerns of this great empire.

"When we contemplate," he says, "our situation in this country; when we reflect that we are governing a population of many millions, to whom our language is unknown; whose religion, habits, manners, usages and prejudices, wholly differ from our own; no argument would seem requisite to prove that the diffusion of the benefits and blessings of a British administration among these our subjects must essentially depend on the degree in which the power of communication with the natives of India is possessed by the public officers employed in the various branches of this great and complicated government. Splendid as has been the career of our dominion, prosperous as has been the conduct of our internal concerns, who will allege that no advantages have been lost, no evils have been incurred, which a skilful use of the powers of language might not have secured and prevented?

"Who will say that improved means of direct intercourse with our subjects are not indispensably required to co-operate with the||enactment and administration of salutary laws for the purpose of diffusing the knowledge and the practice of those principles of conduct which have a tendency to exalt the standard of national character, to diminish the prevalence of immorality and crime, and to promote the general welfare and happiness of the inhabitants of these territories? Who will maintain that far greater advances in the attainment of such important purposes might not long since have been made, if the existing facilities of Oriental study and acquirement had in early times enabled the Company's servants to arrive at that proficiency which is now so generally attained?"

These observations are prefectly just, but something further might be added on the subject. The progressive extension and prosperity of the British dominions in India has been founded mainly on its military and political power; but, in the military line and the highest departments of government, circumstances rarely fail to generate the qualifications required. All ages and countries have produced warriors and statesmen. A few great and illustrious individuals, such as we may suppose might be formed out of the number of Englishmen sent to the east, might be sufficient so to animate the whole body of their countrymen, and so skilfully to manage the natives, as to acquire and maintain enormous possessions against Mahometan and Indian competitors. But it is a very different thing when the question is no longer about the acquisition and maintenance of empire, but the administration of justice and of a good internal government to sixty millions of subjects. Here the few men of great talents, who will always be found among a certain number, are comparatively without power. They cannot act without instruments. These instruments must necessarily be a considerable body of civil servants, not only possessing the means of easy communication with the natives, but of improved understandings, of acquired knowledge, and of habits of steady application and industry. When it is recollected that there is no judge on the bench in England who is not of mature age, and has not shown himself for many years eminent among a number of eminent competitors, it is difficult to conceive that the judicial department in India should be in any degree adequately filled. And though it might be allowed that out of the number supplied from England in the civil and military line, according to the former system, India would never be deficient in persons fit to command in the field, or advise in the cabinet; yet that such a body, so collected, should furnish a sufficient number of persons competent to conduct ably and efficiently the whole internal administration of so great and populous a country, seems next to an impossibility. Nothing, then, can be more futile||than the argument in favor of the former system, derived from the progressive extension of our power in the east. In fact the past and present internal state of India directly contradict the arguments.

Before the period of the establishment of the Board of Controul and the commencement of the government of Lord Cornwallis, however wonderful might have been the progress of our power, the internal prosperity of the provinces in our possession was generally considered to be on the decline; and, even since that period, the commercial, financial, and territorial prosperity of British India, has certainly not kept pace with the brilliant career of its arms and councils. Considering the long peace which Bengal has enjoyed under the protection of these arms, its cultivation, wealth, and population, have not increased so much as might naturally have been expected; and not only would it be rash to affirm, as Mr. Edmonstone intimates, that no advantages have been lost in consequence of the deficient knowledge of the Company's servants, but it would probably be quite safe to assert, that the interests of the Company and the happiness and prosperity of their Indian subjects must have suffered materially from this cause; that they suffer in some degree still; but that they suffered much more, antecedently to the commencement of the improved system of education, when the number of those who attained to any degree of proficiency in the languages was extremely confined; when, according to Mr. Edmonstone, the *Arabic* and *Sanscrit* could boast only of a few occasional votaries; when the proportion of the servants of the Company who acquired a knowledge of the *Persian* language was comparatively inconsiderable, and the general standard of proficiency in that language was extremely low; when, unassisted by a Moonshee, few were capable of executing the

ordinary business of translating from Persian into
English, and still fewer were able to perform the con-
verse of that operation with any grammatical correctness, without the same assistance; when the number of those who were adequately conversant in the
Hindoostanee was extremely limited, and the language
of *Bengal* was almost generally neglected and unknown. Mr. Edmonstone then adds, "how essential,
how extensive, has been the change in all these
respects!"

It might naturally be expected that the defects of
the former system would be the least conspicuous in
the acquisition of the languages; and that an early
removal to India, and an early employment in some
subordinate official situation, would not have been
very disadvantageous in this respect, however disadvantageous it would be, as directly stated by Lord
Wellesley, with a view to the attainments necessary
in the higher departments of the service.||

But it appears, that even in the languages, with
the exception of a few self-taught individuals, the
deficiency was very great. What then must it have
been in the other qualifications necessary for the
internal administration of a great country?

When to these statements of Mr. Edmonstone, and
the inferences which follow from them, we add the
distinct declaration of the Marquis Wellesley, before
quoted, respecting the insufficient qualifications of the
great body of the civil servants, it is abundantly evident that an improved education for the civil service
of the Company was not an imaginary and theoretical,

but a real and practical want—a want which, in some way or other, required unquestionably to be supplied.

SECTION III.—*In order to secure the attainment of the qualifications necessary for the civil servants of the Company, is an appropriate establishment necessary? and should it be of the nature of a School or a College?*

The Marquis Wellesley, after dwelling upon the qualifications necessary for the civil service of the Company, observes that it is unnecessary to enter into an examination of facts to prove that no system of education, study, or discipline, now exists either in Europe or India, founded on the principles or directed to the objects which he had described; and his opinion of the necessity of an appropriate institution was fully evinced by the grand collegiate establishment which he founded at Fort William.

It is well known that this establishment, in its full extent, was not sanctioned by the Court of Directors. The main ground of their rejection of it they stated to be the enormous and indefinite expense in which it must involve the Company, which they considered as too great for the actual state of their affairs. They paid high compliments to the liberal and enlightened spirit and great ability of the Marquis, though they only expressed their approbation of parts of his plan. They acknowledged, however, the necessity of an improved education for their civil servants, but seemed to think that this object might be effectually accomplished by an enlarged seminary for Oriental learning at Calcutta, combined with an improved system of education in Europe, suitable to the sphere of life in which their civil servants were intended to move.

None of the old establishments in England offered such a system of education. The great public schools, which, upon the Marquis Wellesley's plan of an university education in Calcutta, would have answered perfectly well for the European part of the educa-|| tion till fifteen or sixteen, were evidently insufficient when the Indian part of the education was to be confined exclusively to the Oriental languages, and conducted without any system of discipline.

A regular course of study at Oxford and Cambridge would evidently detain the young men too long in England, and would defer the commencement of their Indian career till the age of twenty-two or twenty-three; a period, which is considered as decidedly objectionable, both with respect to the greater difficulty they would find in accommodating themselves to Indian manners and habits, and to the necessarily later period of life at which they could expect to return to their native country with a competency.

Whatever difficulties or objections, therefore, might attend an institution exclusively applied to the education of the young persons destined to go out to India as writers, such an appropriate institution seemed to be necessarily required by the specific wants of the Company.

But if an appropriate establishment was necessary, the nature of the object to be attained obviously dictated the propriety of its assuming a collegiate form.

At the time that the establishment in Hertfordshire was founded, the plan of general education projected by the Marquis Wellesley at the college in Calcutta had been given up, and the lectures were confined exclusively to the Oriental languages. It was necessary, therefore, with a view to the qualifications acknowledged to be required in the service, to commence a plan of more general study in England; and for this purpose a school was unfit.

At a school which the boys would leave at an early age, little more could be learnt with advantage than at the usual seminaries of the country. If the age of proceeding to India was in general not later than sixteen, there would certainly be ample time for the acquisition of the Oriental languages in that country before a writer could be employed, or, at least, before he ought to be employed, in any official situation beyond that of copying-clerk; and the advantage which he would gain by commencing the Oriental languages at school would be so trifling as not nearly to counterbalance the time employed on them.

It will hardly be contended, that boys under the age of sixteen are fit to commence that course of general reading which may be considered as appropriate to their future destination; and an attempt to introduce such a system would inevitably occasion the complete sacrifice of classical studies, with scarcely a possibility of substituting any thing in their stead but that mercantile education, so strongly reprobated by Lord Wellesley.

With regard to conduct,—the strict discipline and constant su-||perintendence of a school would be but a bad preparation for the entire independence, and complete freedom from all restraint, which would await them on their arrival at Calcutta; and as long as they continue to proceed to India at the age of school-boys, whether they are taken from an appropriate establishment, or from the common schools of the country, nothing is done towards removing or mitigating the dangers arising from this cause.

If to these considerations be added the objections which have been made to an appropriate establishment for India, as tending to generate something like an Indian caste (objections which might have some weight if the exclusive education commenced as early as twelve or thirteen), it may safely be concluded that any expenditure of the Company in an *appropriate school* would not only be entirely wasted, but would probably be the means of giving them servants of less powerful minds, and inferior general abilities, than if they had been taken promiscuously from the common schools of the country.

To accomplish the particular object proposed some institution was required, which was adapted to form the understandings of persons above the age of mere boys, where a more liberal system of discipline might be introduced; and where, instead of being kept to their studies solely by the fear of immediate observation and punishment, they might learn to be influenced by the higher motives of the love of distinction and the fear of disgrace, and to depend for success upon their own diligence and self-controul; upon the power of regulating their own time and attention; and on habits of systematic and persevering application, when out of the presence of their teachers. Nothing but an institution approaching in some degree to a college, and possessing some degree of college liberty, could either generate such habits, or properly develop the different characters of the young persons educated in it; and mark with sufficient precision the industrious and the indolent, the able and the deficient, the well-disposed and the turbulent. Nothing, in short, but an institution at which the students would remain till eighteen or nineteen, could be expected properly to prepare them for the acquisition of those high qualifications, which had been stated from the best authority to be necessary for a very large portion of the civil servants of the Company, in order to enable them to discharge their various and important duties with credit to themselves and advantage to the service.

Yet, in spite of these obvious reasons, which seemed to settle the question at once in favor of a college, there were many who preferred a school, as there were many who would have greatly preferred the having neither the one nor the other. The motives for this latter preference were sufficiently intelligible.||

Besides the argument for leaving things as they are, which so many persons are always ready to apply on all occasions, it was certain that any system of education at a particular establishment, which was made a necessary qualification for an appointment to India, must tend rather to diminish the value of the patronage of the Directors. In the first place, the expense of the education would generally be considered by the parents and guardians of the young person appointed as a drawback upon the advantage received. And, secondly, the chance that, from inability or misconduct, the appointment might not be confirmed, would be a consideration of a nature to have great weight with those who, it is to be feared, sometimes wish to send out a son, or other connexion, to India, whose conduct and attainments do not promise a very fortunate career at home.

It is evident that most of the reasons which would determine many persons to prefer the old system to any kind of establishment whatever, for the education of the civil servants of the Company, would determine them to prefer a school to a college, if it were necessary to choose between the two evils. They would be aware that a young person must be educated somewhere, before he reaches the earliest age at which he can be sent to India, and it would not make much difference in expense whether he was educated at a common school or one established by the Company. The early conclusion of his education, and the early period of his proceeding to India, would remove, either wholly, or in a great degree, the objections on the score of expense. They would probably presume also, that as, at a school, the boys would be kept in order by the birch, there would be much less danger of the loss of an appointment. In this, however, they would probably find themselves mistaken. Birch supports discipline, only because it is itself supported by the fear of expulsion: remove this fear, and the effect of the rod will soon cease. In almost all cases, the physical force is on the side of the gov-

erned; and few youths of sixteen would submit to be
flogged if they did not know that immediate expulsion
would be the consequence of their refusal. If the East-
India Company had an establishment for the education of boys from thirteen to sixteen, there is great
reason to believe that without the usual gradation of
ages from nine and ten upwards, and with any hesitation in resorting to the punishment of expulsion on
all the usual occasions, it would be scarcely possible
to enforce proper obedience; and the rod itself would
probably be one of the principal causes of resistance
and rebellion.

A school therefore, besides excluding at once the
great object in view—an education fitted for the
higher offices of the government—seemed to present
no one intelligible advantage over a col-||lege, but that
of diminishing, in a smaller degree, the patronage of
the Directors. This advantage, to the honor of the
Court, was not regarded, in comparison of the advantages which their Indian territories might derive
from the improved education of their civil servants;
and a college was determined upon.

One of the great objections urged by Adam Smith
against the government of an exclusive Company is,
that their interests, as a sovereign, are generally considered as subordinate to their interests as individuals,
or as a body of merchants. In the establishment of
the East-India college, the feelings of the sovereign
conspicuously predominated; and the public did
justice to the disinterested motives and the enlarged
and enlightened views which prompted the decision.

SECTION IV.—*Should the appropriate establishment formed by the East-India Company be in England or India? or should there be establishments in both countries?*

The practical part of this question has been already decided in the Court of Directors by their establishment of an appropriate college in England for the education of their civil servants, and by their resolution to confine the object of their college in Calcutta exclusively to the Oriental languages. But the question may at any time be revived. Feeling present inconveniences and evils from the establishment in England, the Court may again think of reverting to a system of general education in Calcutta. And it may be useful to state, preparatory to any such experiment, the evils and inconveniencies which are likely to result from a regular college in India.

In the first place, it is well known that the expense would be beyond all comparison greater than in England, probably, at the least, six or seven times as great; and though the object of an improved education is of such paramount importance that it is the last quarter in which expense should be considered, yet, if this object can be effectually accomplished upon a more economical plan, there can be no doubt of the duty and propriety of adopting it.

In England the most able instructors may be obtained in all the departments of knowledge and literature at salaries quite moderate, compared with those which would be necessary to induce men of the same attainments to afford their assistance in

India; and if to these superior salaries be added the much heavier Pension List that would inevitably accompany them, the difference would be still farther increased.||

In England every part of a collegiate establishment, the buildings, the table, the attendance, &c. &c. may be kept within very moderate bounds; but in India, where a certain style of living seems to be expected from all the Company's servants, this would be extremely difficult, and the expenditure under all these heads would be upon a much larger and more extended scale.

In England, at the college now established, not only the personal expenses of the students are supported by their parents and friends, but a hundred guineas a year are paid towards their education. If the two years from sixteen to eighteen were spent at a college in India, the students would of course be paid the salaries of writers from the time of their arrival; and, reckoning the average of the yearly admissions at forty, eighty persons more than at present would be living upon the Indian revenue. The salaries of the junior writers are 300 rupees a month, or about 450l. a year; and on this article alone, therefore, the present system saves 36,000l. a year to the Company.

It may be said, perhaps, that it is not to be wished that the expenses of the necessary education of the Company's servants should fall so heavily upon their parents and connexions, and that it would sometimes be desirable to give appointments to persons whose families could not easily support such an expense. That such instances may occur there can be no doubt;

but, as a general rule, there can be as little doubt that
the preparatory education for official situations not
only usually is, but ought to be, supported by the
families of the candidates themselves, and in the particular case in question it is highly beneficial to the
Company's service that the candidates for writerships
should be taken almost exclusively from that class of
society which may be supposed capable of paying the
expenses of a good common education. There is
reason to believe, from the information of residents
in India, and from the qualifications of some of the
students who even now present themselves for admission to the college in Hertfordshire, that before its
establishment persons were occasionally sent out to
India so extremely ill-suited to the situations in which
they were likely to be placed, both from their previous
habits, and the kind of education they had received,
that it was scarcely possible to employ them without
injury to the service.

The college in India, established upon the Marquis
Wellesley's plan, cost in the first year about 76,000l.
For the two following years the estimates were about
48,000l., but the change of plan prevented the correctness of them from being ascertained. In neither
calculation, however, were the additional salaries of
eighty students included. These salaries, it was considered, would be paid equally, whether the writers
resided in the college, or were||less usefully employed
in some subordinate offices; and this was certainly
true; but the whole of this expense would of course be
wed upon the supposition that the two years from
sixteen to eighteen were spent in England.

The expense of the college in England, beyond what is paid by the students, and independently of the building, may be estimated at between nine and ten thousand a year, so that the expenses of the college in India would altogether at the least be six or seven times as great as that in England.

Secondly, in point of regularity of conduct and personal expenses, the advantage possessed by the college in England will scarcely appear less marked than its advantage in point of economy.[1]

It is generally acknowledged that the young men who go out as writers to India have the power of borrowing money almost to any extent from natives, who speculate upon their future rise in the service; and during the early part of their residence in Calcutta it is but too common to indulge in an expenditure greatly beyond their incomes. They find themselves besides the members of a privileged caste; and the almost arbitrary controul which they exercise over the persons whom they chiefly see about them, must have a necessary tendency to foster their caprices, and render them impatient of authority. If to these causes of irregularity we add the seductions of a luxurious climate, and consider at the same time the critical age from sixteen to nineteen at which they are at first exposed to these temptations, it is difficult to conceive a more dangerous ordeal. The deficient discipline of our schools and universities in England has

---

[1] I say this with confidence, notwithstanding the clamour that has lately been made in the Court of Proprietors, and in the public prints, about the irregularities prevailing in the East India college.

often been the subject of complaint; but it may safely be pronounced, that if our youth from sixteen to nineteen were exposed to the same temptations as they would be during a three-years' residence at a college in Calcutta, their discipline would not admit of a comparison with what it is at present.

But it is not only to be expected, according to all general principles, that violations of any regular system of academical discipline in India would be much more frequent than in a similar institution in England, but the means of punishment, when such offences had been committed, would be much more difficult and embarrassing.

It is well known that in all places of education for gentlemen the efficacy of minor punishments is only supported by the final appeal to expulsion. Even in military seminaries, where strict||personal confinement is frequently applied, expulsion and dismissal from the service are the punishments for continued acts of contumacy and rebellion; and in civil institutions, where the intermediate punishments can scarcely be made so effective, this final appeal is still more absolutely necessary. But in India the expelled students, though not perhaps subsequently promoted to any lucrative situation, would still continue to receive the salaries of writers according to their standing; and if the old plan of sending youths to India without any kind of previous selection or examination were reverted to, and they were never sent back, the number might in time become so considerable as to be a serious weight on the Company's finances.

At a preparatory institution in England, if a young

man, either from absolute want of capacity, from determined idleness, or any violent act of contumacy, loses his promised appointment to a writership, and is excluded from the service, there are various other lines of exertion open to him. Some employments may be found at home even for a very feeble capacity; the most determined academical idleness till nineteen or twenty, may yield to the pressure of strong necessity and real business; and a young man of talents, who from temper, caprice, or any other cause, had been guilty of some violent act of contumacy, might rise to the top of his profession as a lawyer, a soldier, a sailor, or a merchant.

In India there is only one line of employment, and that is the Company's service. A youth, who is expelled from a college in India for any of the causes above enumerated, is expelled by the same authority which disposes of all Indian appointments. If this same authority, after a short interval, promotes him to office even on the supposition that he is then fit for it, an expulsion from the college would come to be considered as of little importance, and its discipline would soon be destroyed.

In the last public examination at the college in India, of which the account has arrived, five students were expelled. Notwithstanding the opportunities of instruction afforded to them, and the repeated warnings they had received during a protracted stay at Calcutta, they had not acquired such a knowledge of two Oriental languages as would enable them to pass the examination necessary to qualify them for any official situation.

If a test be established any where, either in India
or England, and the examination be conducted conscientiously, it may be laid down as a certain consequence that *some*, out of a considerable number of
young men, taken without any selection, will fail. If,
besides the passing of such a test, obedience be required to a code of academical regulations, however
mildly administered, a greater||number will undoubt-
edly fail. And the question is, whether it is not very
much better that these failures should take place in
England, where various other lines of life besides the
Company's service are open, than in India, where they
must remain unemployed, a burden to themselves and
the Company, or be sent back to Europe at a very
heavy expense, and at a more advanced age; or, what
is much the worst of the three, be employed when not
properly qualified, to the manifest injury of the Company's service and the interest of their Indian dominions; or even, if qualified, to the utter subversion of
that code of academical laws which had been established as necessary to the proper training and education of their civil servants?

It is certainly conceivable that parents in narrow
circumstances may wish to get their children off their
hands as early as possible, with little regard of the
consequences to the Company. But even such views
would, probably, be defeated on the establishment of
a college for a three-years' course of academical education in Calcutta. As it has appeared that, according
to all general principles, more failures might be expected in India than in England, it would soon be
found necessary to send back those who failed to

their friends in England. It is understood that this measure was once proposed by Lord Minto, in the case of some students who had resided nearly three years in the college without making a progress in any language. The proposition, it is said, was rejected by the Court at home. But if the number of writers so situated were to accumulate in a considerable degree, the proposition for returning them could not be rejected without obviously and grossly sacrificing the Company's interests, and they would then be sent back at a later age, and under much less favourable circumstances for the commencement of a new career of life, than if they had failed at a college in England. But whether this measure would be adopted or not, it must be allowed that those who look solely to a provision for their children cannot be considered as disinterested judges in a question of this kind. And it is scarcely conceivable that any really disinterested friend to the good government of India, and the prosperity and credit of the Company, should not say that, if failures must be calculated upon, it is far better, under all the circumstances of the case, that they should take place in England than in India.

Thirdly, in point of efficiency, it can hardly be doubted, that the foundation of a general education would be better laid in England than in India. The most important period in the education of a young man is the period in which he commences a more general course of reading than that which is pursued at schools; and it is of the utmost consequence that this period should be||passed under circumstances favourable to habits of study and industrious exertion. But it is not easy to conceive a more unfavourable time for the formation of these habits, and the commencement of new and difficult studies, than the two or three years immediately succeeding the transition from a common school in England to an university in India, at the age of sixteen. Suddenly possessed of an unusual command of money, surrounded by natives devoted to his will, tempted to indulgences of all kinds by the novel forms in which they present themselves, and discouraged from severe application by the enfeebling effects of the climate, he must possess a very steady and unusual degree of resolution to begin a course of law, history, political economy, and natural philosophy, and to continue his classical studies, at the very same time that he is required as his paramount duty, and the immediate passport to an official situation, to make himself master of two or three Oriental languages. Such a course of general reading may, undoubtedly, be pursued in India at a future time by individuals, during the intervals of official occupation; but it may be considered as certain that, except, perhaps, in a few rare instances, little or no attention would be paid to these studies in a three-years' residence at Calcutta from sixteen to nineteen, and that, if such a general education be necessary, the foundation of it must be laid in England.

The Marquis Wellesley's college in India had not, it must be allowed, a fair trial. It is hardly just, therefore, to quote it as an example: but, as far as a judgment might be formed of the effects of such an establishment from the manner in which it commenced, it tends strongly to confirm what has been said of the great difficulty of establishing a regular system of discipline, and beginning with success a plan of more general study in an university at Calcutta. The state of the college with regard to discipline is well known, and need not to be entered upon; and, though other lectures besides those in the Oriental languages were given, they were scarcely ever attended. It has been stated, indeed, by those who have acted as professors at the college in Calcutta, as well as by those who have gone through it as students, that, however great are the advantages it affords in the study of the Oriental languages, they see no prospect of its ever becoming a place of regular collegiate discipline, and of efficient general education.

But a general course of study, however necessary to the education of those who are to fill the judicial, the financial, and the diplomatic departments in India, or assist in the administration of the Government as Members in Council, is not alone sufficient: and the highest intellectual endowments would be of little avail without a knowledge of the Oriental languages. A certain know-||ledge, therefore, of these languages, must always be considered as a *sine quâ non* in the appointment to official situations. This knowledge, will, indeed, do little without any other combined with it; but no knowledge can do any thing without the means of communication with the natives.

Two objects therefore are to be kept in view; one of the highest utility, and the other of paramount necessity. As a foundation of general knowledge is best laid in the West, and the necessary languages are best acquired in the East, it seems highly probable that two establishments, one in England, and the other in India, may be required to accomplish most effectively the objects in view:—the English establishment to give as good a general education as can be communicated within the age of 18 or 19, with some instruction in the rudiments of the Oriental languages; and the Indian establishment to be confined exclusively to these languages, and particularly to act as a final test, as far as languages go, of qualification for office.

It has been found, by experience, that those young men, who go out to India tolerably well grounded in the rudiments of the Oriental languages, can, without difficulty, pass the necessary test within the year, and many of them pass it in six months. Upon this plan, therefore, the time taken up in the preparatory education for the civil service would scarcely be greater than upon the Marquis Wellesley's plan. But, even if it were somewhat greater, it is probable that the interests, both of the service and of individuals, would be promoted by this change. It is certainly the opinion of some of the writers themselves, that, even since the establishment of both the colleges, they are advanced to important situations in the judicial line at too early, rather than too late an age. And it by no means follows that the going out to India a year or two later implies a proportionally later return.

The period in which a fortune is made, ought not to be dated from the time of arrival in India, but from the time at which accumulation commences. And, if a year or two more spent in Europe be employed in such a manner as to send the young writer out, not only with superior qualifications for office, but with a greater degree of general prudence, he is likely to begin saving sooner, and will, perhaps, return with a fortune at an earlier age than if he had been exposed from the age of fifteen or sixteen to a three years' residence at Calcutta, and the heavy debt which too frequently accompanies it.

No time therefore is really lost either to the service or to individuals by the period devoted to education in England. And, as the expenses of the Indian college, in its present state, without buildings, without a table, without a Principal and Professors of||European literature, and general management, and with the limited number arising from only a year, or a year and a half's residence, may be kept within very moderate bounds, there can be no doubt, on the whole, that the present system of education in the two colleges, compared with a regular university course in India, is much more economical, most efficient with regard to general knowledge, and exposed to fewer difficulties in point of discipline and personal dissipation and extravagance.

SECTION V.—*Does it appear that the College actually established in Hertfordshire is upon a plan calculated to supply that part of the appropriate education of the civil servants of the Company which ought to be completed in England?*

When the Court of Directors declined sanctioning the collegiate establishment proposed by the Marquis Wellesley, they did not hesitate to acknowledge the necessity of an improved education for their civil servants; and it was for the specific purpose of securing to them such an improved education before they left England, without detaining them till the usual age at which an university course finishes (to which detention the Marquis had objected), that the Court of Directors founded the institution in Hertfordshire.

At this institution the students commence a course of more general instruction than is to be found at schools, nearly at the same period that they were to commence it in India according to Lord Wellesley's plan, and *yet* proceed to their destination at eighteen or nineteen, an age at which the constitution is better fortified against the Indian climate than two or three years earlier, but not sufficiently advanced to be open to those objections urged by Lord Wellesley against a detention till twenty-one or twenty-two.

In the East-India college, so constituted, the plan upon which the system of discipline and instruction is conducted seems to be well calculated to answer the purpose in view. Every candidate for admission into the college is required to produce a testimonial from his schoolmaster, and to pass an examination in Greek, Latin, and arithmetic, before the Principal and Professors. This previous examination at once prevents persons from offering themselves who have not received the usual school-education of the higher classes of society; and those who offer themselves, and are found deficient, are remanded till another period of admission.

The lectures of the different Professors in the college are given in a manner to make previous preparation necessary, and to encourage most effectually habits of industry and application. In‖their substance they embrace the important subjects of classical literature, the Oriental languages, the elements of mathematics and natural philosophy, the laws of England, general history, and political economy.

At the commencement of the institution it was feared by some persons that this variety would too much distract the attention of the students at the age of sixteen or seventeen, and prevent them from making a satisfactory progress in any department. But instances of distinguished success in many departments at the same time have proved that these fears were without foundation; and that this variety has not only been useful to them in rendering a methodical arrangement of their hours of study more necessary, but has decidedly contributed to enlarge, invigorate, and mature their understandings.

On all the important subjects above enumerated, examinations take place twice in the year, at the end of each term. These examinations last above a fortnight. They are conducted upon the plan of the great public and collegiate examinations in the universities, particularly at Cambridge, with such further improvements as experience has suggested. The questions given are framed with a view to ascertain the degree of progress and actual proficiency in each particular department on the subjects studied during the preceding term; and the answers, in all cases which will admit of it, are given in writing, in the presence of the professors, and without the possibility of a reference to books. After the examination in any particular department is over, the Professor in that department reviews at his leisure all the papers that he has received, and places, as nearly as he can, each individual in the numerical order of his relative merit, and in certain divisions implying his degree of positive merit. These arrangements are all subject to the controul of the whole collegiate body. They require considerable time and attention, and are executed with scrupulous care and strict impartiality.

Besides the classifications above mentioned, medals, prizes of books, and honorary distinctions, are awarded to those who are the heads of classes, or as high as second, third, fourth, or fifth, in two, three, four, or five departments.

These means of exciting emulation and industry have been attended with great success. Though there are some, unquestionably, on whom motives of this kind will not, or cannot, operate, and with whom, therefore, little can be done; yet, a more than usual proportion seem to be animated by a strong desire, accompanied by corresponding efforts, to make a progress in the various studies proposed to them.

Those who have come to college tolerably good scholars, have||often, during their stay of two years, made such advances in the classical department as would have done them great credit, if they had devoted to it the main part of their time; while the contemporary honours which they have obtained in other departments have sufficiently proved that their attention was not confined to one study: and many, who had come from public and private schools at sixteen, with such low classical attainments as appeared to indicate a want either of capacity or application, have shown by their subsequent progress, even in the classical department, and still more by their distinguished exertions in others, that a new field and new stimulants had wrought a most beneficial change in their feelings and habits, and had awakened energies of which they were before scarcely conscious.

There are four or five of the Professors thoroughly conversant with University examinations, who can take upon themselves to affirm that they have never witnessed a greater proportion of various and successful exertion in the course of their academical experience than has appeared at some of the examinations at the East-India college.

With regard to the discipline of the establishment, it will be readily allowed that it has not been, in all its parts, so successful. It is well known that disturbances have occasionally taken place, which, at the moment, have shown, in a considerable body of the students, a total disregard of the rules and regulations of the college. The principal causes of these disturbances will be the subject of inquiry in the next section; but it is proper to observe here, that the public would form a most incorrect notion of the general state and character of the discipline, and the general conduct of the students, if they were to draw hasty inferences from these temporary ebullitions. When they have subsided, few traces of their past existence are to be found; and in common times the whole business of the college proceeds with a degree of decency, order, and decorum, which has often been the admiration of strangers, and would be perfectly satisfactory to every competent judge.

In their moral conduct, the students of the East-India college may be advantageously compared with those of either University, or the senior part of any of our great public schools; and they are rather singularly free, than otherwise, from the prevailing vices which beset young men of seventeen, eighteen, and nineteen, particularly when collected together in a large body.

It is from such comparisons, and the general results which appear in after-life, and not from individuals, or individual offences, that any rational judgment can be formed of a place of education.||

On the whole, perhaps it is not too much to assert, that, taking literary and moral character together, a considerable proportion of the students of the East-India college, who have proceeded to India, have left it with more improved understandings, a greater quantity of useful knowledge, fitted for the early discharge of public business, and more steady habits of application and good conduct, than could be found among any set of young men taken in the same way, and at the same age, from any place of public education in Europe: and *some of them* with such distinguished attainments already acquired, such means of acquiring more, and such fixed habits of honor and integrity, that no situation, however high, would be above their powers or beyond their deserts.

It will be asked, however, as the main question, whether the good effects which may be presumed to result from the establishment in England have practically been perceived and acknowledged by competent judges in India? To this question an answer may be decidedly given in the affirmative. The young men who arrive at the Calcutta college from the college in England are not examined respecting their progress in general knowledge. On this point, therefore, there can be no specific testimony. But with regard to *general conduct and character,* and such a knowledge of the Oriental languages as greatly to abridge the period of study at Calcutta, the testimony is most explicit, and from the highest authority.

In 1810, Lord Minto, after having noticed particularly a certain number of students who had greatly distinguished themselves, adds, "It is with peculiar pleasure that I do a further justice to the Hertford college, by remarking, that the official reports and returns of our college will show the students who have been translated from Hertford to Fort William to stand honorably distinguished for regular attendance, —for obedience to the statutes and discipline of the college,—for orderly and decorous demeanour,—for moderation in expense, and consequently in the amount of their debt;—and, in a word, for those decencies of conduct which denote men well born, and characters well trained. I make this observation with the more satisfaction, as I entertain an earnest wish to find it proved that the preliminary tuition and general instruction afforded to the succeeding generations of the Company's servants at Hertford will be found of more *extensive* (I should be disposed to say, more *valuable*) influence even for India, than a greater or smaller degree of proficiency in a language or two of the East can prove at that early period."

In 1812, the following passage occurs in a letter from the College Council of Fort William to the Governor-General in Council,||dated December 29, and recorded in the Bengal Public Consultations of the 1st of April, 1814:—

"We take the liberty of repeating in this place the observations made by the Right Honorable the Visitor, in his speech, pronounced at the Disputation, holden 22d September, 1810, that the improvement (a very great and general one) which we have thought ourselves warranted in asserting, has been very conspicuous in the conduct of the students, who have passed through the college at Hertford. We trust and believe that this is no accidental circumstance; but at all events the fact is, in our opinion, certain, that, due regard being paid to numbers, no similar institution can afford a greater proportion of young men more distinguished by the manners of gentlemen, and general correctness and propriety of deportment, than the present students of the college at Fort William."

At nearly the same period this improvement in the general conduct of the students is spoken of as an acknowledged fact, in a letter from Captain Roebuck to the College Council, at Fort William, dated Nov. 10, 1812, and recorded on the Consultations before mentioned:—"As I believe (he says) it is generally admitted as a fact that the students now in college, compared with former years, are much steadier in every respect (which is, perhaps, owing to their pre-

vious education at Hertford College), I can account,"
&c. &c.

At the Public Disputation in 1815, Mr. Edmonstone, who acted as Visitor in the absence of Lord Moira, after adverting to the objections that had sometimes been made to the college, on the ground of the conduct of the students, observes—"To whatever extent the change might have been justly applicable at some period of the institution, I have the satisfaction to know that, at the present time, instances of deviation from the maxims and rules of prudence and propriety (for such must always exist in every large association) are exceptions to the general system of conduct observable among the students of the college." He then goes on to say—"This gratifying improvement may, perhaps, be traced to sources *beyond this establishment"*—evidently alluding to the acknowledged effects of the institution in England.

These public testimonies from the college at Calcutta are confirmed by the accounts of individuals who have returned from India within the last six or seven years, who agree in stating that what has been sometimes called the New School of Writers at Calcutta is very superior indeed, both in conduct and attainments, to those who were sent out upon the old system.

The period when the conduct of the junior servants of the||Company appears to have been most marked with dissipation and irregularity was in the interval between 1801 and 1808 or 1809, when great numbers were collected together in Calcutta at the early ages of sixteen and seventeen, without being subjected to a regular system of discipline, as intended by Lord Wellesley; and the marked improvement so generally acknowledged may fairly be attributed to the establishment of an intermediate place of education in England, which prevents the sudden removal of a boy of fifteen or sixteen from the strict restraints of a school to the dangerous liberty of a residence at Calcutta.

At the college in England each student has a separate room, in which he breakfasts, drinks tea, and prepares his lectures. This mode of living gives him the opportunity of choosing his own society, and teaches him the habit of regulating his own time; while the discipline is still suited to an age two or three years younger than the average age at the universities; and industry and application are encouraged by every moral incitement which can stimulate the youthful mind. A habit of study so acquired must be the best possible preparation for a residence at Calcutta, and the best preservative against its allurements. And, though it cannot be expected that all should acquire these invaluable habits, yet much is done if they are acquired by a considerable body. Besides, all will be detained in England till eighteen or nineteen—an age when they may be fairly supposed to know better how to conduct themselves in a situation in which they are subjected to no discipline. And, owing to this same detention, all will reside a much shorter time at the college in Calcutta, and find themselves surrounded by a much smaller number of associates. These are causes calculated to operate favourably on the whole mass, and not only to lessen the shock of the first transition, but to diminish both the duration and amount of the dangers to which they are exposed.

Under these circumstances it cannot be a matter of surprise that the general conduct of the students at Calcutta should have greatly improved since the establishment of the college in England.

On the effect of the college in England in abridging the period of stay at the college in Calcutta, the testimonies are equally satisfactory.

At the public disputation of 1810, before adverted to, Lord Minto says, "That the studies of Hertford will abridge those of Fort William cannot be doubted. This has already been proved."—He had before indeed observed, that the college of Fort William had already derived some of its most distinguished ornaments from Hertford. "I do not speak," he says, "of the merit to which I now allude in comparison only with that of contemporaries of the present year, but I would place it confidently in parallel with the||best and brightest period of our college." To warrant this homage, justly and impartially paid to the early fruit of the new (not rival, but associate) institution, he names eight students from Hertford, who had eminently distinguished themselves. Of these the average period of stay at the college of Fort William was about a year, although some of them had delayed their going longer than was necessary; and three had acquired a proficiency in no less than four Oriental languages.

In 1811, the documents furnish the means of a more accurate comparison. In that year the number of students which left the Calcutta college qualified for official situations was twenty, of whom the number from the college in Hertfordshire was twelve, *viz.*

Six who left the college after six months' residence.
Two .... after eight months.
One .... after nine months.
One .... after two years.
Two .... after three years.

The number of students who left the Calcutta college at the same time, but never were at the college in Hertfordshire, was eight, *viz.*

Three after a residence of two years and a quarter.
One .... of three years.
One .... of three years and a quarter.
Two .... of four years.
One .... of four years and a half.

In the one case, the average stay is about ten months; in the other, three years and two months.

It will be unnecessary to go through all the different years; indeed, the means for so doing are not at hand. They will, of course, be subject to considerable variations, arising from the natural variations to be expected at different times in the mass of talent and industry in the college, and probably in some years the average period of stay may be as much as a year and a half. The summary of the last year of which the account has arrived is as follows: Of eighteen students who left the college, six had resided only six months; two, ten months; eight, about a year and a half; and the other two, three and a half and four and a half years.

In most years one or two are to be found, who, either from inability or idleness, make no progress in the languages. They are detained in consequence a considerable time, and are generally involved deeply in debt. It would unquestionably be much better for the service, and probably for the individuals themselves, if they||had never gone out; and, as their characters are generally pretty well known previous to the natural time of their departure, the authorities of the college in England ought to be allowed, quietly, and without clamour and opposition, as a regular and very important part of their duty to the Company, to refuse their certificates.

Such cases, however, appear to be quite as rare as could possibly be expected; and the very short period in which the great body of the students from Hertford college acquire the requisite proficiency in two languages, and many of them high distinctions in three or four, sufficiently proves that a foundation in these languages laid in England, and a power thus given of pursuing the study of them during the passage, has a most marked effect in abridging the period of stay at Calcutta.

Lord Moira, at the public disputation of 1814, alludes to the considerable progress made by Mr. Stirling in the Oriental languages prior to his entry at the college by studying at Hertford, and during his voyage to India: and to this, in part, he says, is to be attributed the extraordinary short period in which such extensive knowledge and attainments seemed to have been gained. Mr. Stirling had only resided in India six months; and in fact it appears, that in almost every year a considerable proportion of the students of Fort William, who have passed through the East-India college at home, attain the required qualifications in that short time; and among these are generally to be found some of the most distinguished proficients in the Oriental languages. Lord Moira afterwards observes,—"This is not a seminary, at which the students in general are to be taught the first rudiments of the Eastern languages. It has become, like our Universities at home, a public institution, affording those advantages necessary to perfect the knowledge of the different branches of Oriental literature." These expressions certainly imply a tolerable foundation in the Oriental languages brought from England. An idea seems to have prevailed at Calcutta that the college of Fort William might be superseded by the establishment in England; but it may fairly be allowed that the attention paid to the Oriental languages in England neither can, nor ought, to be such as, generally speaking, to prevent the necessity of a much farther progress after the arrival in India, as a qualification for office. When it is considered that the period of residence at the college in England is only two years, it is quite obvious that the whole of that time exclusively devoted to Oriental study would be insufficient for the purpose in question, while, in the attempt to attain it, the main object of the English institution (which unquestionably is, or ought to be, to lay the foundation of a sound and enlarged European education) would be entirely sacrificed.||

Lord Minto, at the public disputation of 1813, speaking of the insufficient knowledge of the Oriental languages acquired at the Hertford college, observes, "It is not to be concluded from thence that the time allotted to attendance on that institution has been unprofitably spent; because *most wisely,* in my opinion, the preliminary education of the Company's young servants is not confined to studies merely Oriental; but, together with the classical instruction of the West (without which no English gentleman is on a level with his fellows), I understand that a foundation of polite literature is laid, and that the door is opened at least, and the pupil's mind attracted, to the elements of useful science; the seeds of which being sown, a taste for intellectual exercise and enjoyment is implanted, which seldom fails to develop and mature these first germs of knowledge at the appointed season."

If, instead of being employed in this way, so justly approved of by Lord Minto, the students at the college in England were to devote their whole attention to the acquisition of an imperfect knowledge of two or three Oriental languages, and, as soon as they arrived in India, were immediately employed up the country in subordinate official situations, it is not easy to conceive a species of education less calculated to improve and enlarge the understanding, and to produce men able and willing to infuse the principles of British justice into a government over sixty millions of Asiatics.

There is nothing, then, which the enlightened friends of good government in India should less wish to see, than the attempt so much deprecated by Lord Minto, in his last speech, of substituting an English education in the Oriental languages for the genuine and practical instruction which is obtained in India; and the English college itself will be perfectly ready to acquiesce in the final opinion given of it by Lord Minto,—that the elementary knowledge acquired there operates sensibly in accelerating the progress of Oriental studies, and abridging the period necessary for a full qualification at the college of Fort William; but that the institution of Hertford college cannot be expected ever to supersede the necessity of maturing and perfecting Oriental knowledge at the college of Fort William.

The true friends of the college in England will be perfectly satisfied that it fully answers its purpose, and supplies that part of the appropriate education of the civil servants of the Company which ought to be completed at home,—if it effects an essential improvement in the conduct and character of the young men sent out to India;—if it considerably shortens the period of their residence in the college at Calcutta, devoted to the acquisition of the Oriental languages; —and if it lays such a foundation of general knowledge as will greatly facilitate the subsequent pursuit of it,||and qualifies a much greater proportion of the civil servants of the Company to discharge with adequate ability the increased and increasing number of high and important trusts which must necessarily be confined to them.

That the college has actually accomplished, in a very considerable degree, the two first of these objects, is clearly proved, it is conceived, by the direct testimonies contained in the foregoing pages. The last object can hardly be the subject of direct testimony; but it may fairly be presumed that this purpose is accomplished, if an enlarged and improved understanding be considered as useful in conducting the administration of a great empire, and if it is known that the studies in the East-India college are of a nature calculated to attain this qualification, and that a progress has been made in these studies fairly proportioned to the time employed upon them.

SECTION VI.—*Are the disturbances which have taken place in the East-India college to be attributed to any radical and necessary evils inherent in its constitution and discipline, or to incidental and temporary causes, which are likely to be removed?*

Some of the difficulties which have been experienced in the government of the college are, perhaps, to a certain extent, inherent in its constitution.

In the first place, an attempt to give a collegiate education, and to place under collegiate discipline persons of an age from two to three years younger than the average age of admission at our universities, may not be in its nature easy. It is generally allowed that the age from fifteen or sixteen to eighteen is the most difficult to govern. It is precisely that period when the character makes the most rapid change in the shortest time. Two or three years at this critical era convert a boy into a man; and any system of discipline intended to apply to the time when this change is taking place, which happens to be the very time of the residence at the East-India college, is likely to be exposed to various and very opposite objections, according as the earlier or the later age is chiefly considered.

At great schools, where boys sometimes stay till they are eighteen, the seniors in age, who are generally at the same time in the highest classes, form a kind of natural aristocracy, which not only may safely and justly be allowed greater liberties and privileges than others, but may be made, and, in fact, are made, of the greatest use as an intermediate authority to assist in the government of the rest.

In the East-India college, on the contrary, on account of the||period of residence being only two years, and some being admitted at eighteen or nineteen as well as at fifteen and sixteen, there is no such natural aristocracy of age, standing, and acquirements; and it is hardly possible either justly to separate the seniors from the juniors, and allow them distinct privileges, or to make effective use of them, as at great schools, in the administration of the discipline.

The second permanent difficulty which the college has to contend with is the chance that some of the young men, whose parents have obtained appointments for them, may be indisposed to the service, and not really wish to go out to India. Such a temper of mind will, of course, naturally indispose them to submit to the discipline of the college, or to profit by the education which it offers to them, and will, at the same time, make them most pernicious and dangerous examples to others.

The Directors have endeavoured to get rid of this evil by exhorting all those who feel indisposed to the service quietly to withdraw from the college. But it is to be feared that this exhortation, though obviously just and proper, will not often have the desired effect. Instances have not been uncommon of a persevering opposition to the regulations of the college, which could only be rationally accounted for by supposing a positive disinclination to the service; and yet, if the student has, in consequence of his irregularities, been sent home for a time to his friends, their influence has generally produced letters containing expressions of the greatest contrition for past offences, the most solemn assurances with respect to future conduct, and the most anxious desire to proceed to India—professions with which the conduct of the student after his return to college has seemed in no respect to correspond. It is to be feared that there are young men who would prefer expulsion, on occasion of some general disturbance, when many are involved, to an open and manly rejection of an appointment which is considered by their parents as so valuable; and these feelings, where they exist, are obviously of a nature to produce a most unfavorable effect upon the discipline.

The third inherent difficulty, which the college has to contend with, is one which at first sight might be thought an advantage, namely, the great interest that each student has at stake, and the consequent severity of the punishment of expulsion. This great severity most naturally produces, both in the governing body in the college, and in the Court of Directors, an extreme unwillingness to resort to it. But the more this unwillingness is perceived, the more advantage will be taken of it, and the more instances will occur of acts of insubordination. It is quite certain that neither of our Universities, nor any of our great schools, could support their discipline for a single year, if they were to show any hesita-||tion in appealing to the punishment of expulsion—if this punishment, in short, were not always ready as an alternative on a refusal to do impositions in the one case, or to submit to corporal correction in the other. But besides regular expulsions, which are resorted to occasionally in all places of education, to support the discipline, it is still more common to desire the parents of boys, whose habits are bad, and who are doing mischief to others, quietly to remove them. In the Universities, and at great schools, such hints are always taken as commands, and it is no doubt a most effectual mode of breaking combinations, and preventing the spread of mischief, without exciting public sensation. But in the East-India college no parent can be persuaded to take a step which involves the loss of an appointment. As valuable property is concerned, it is considered that nothing but some great and overt act of immorality or rebellion can justify such a punishment; and unless some such act can be brought forward, which, of course, in many cases, must be extremely difficult, neither a quiet removal nor regular expulsion takes place; and the unavoidable severities of the penal code thus paralyse the arm of authority. On this ground it may justly be doubted whether the regulation not long since passed by the Court, to exclude from the military, or any other branch of the Company's service, those young men who had been expelled from the college, can be considered as a wise one. The punishment of expulsion at the college was too great before, and this regulation has made it still greater; and if the natural unwillingness of all parties to resort to this punishment should increase from this or any other cause, rather than diminish from a sense of duty to India and to the public; the great power of the Directors over the young men at their college, which, if properly managed, might secure the most beneficial results, will be converted into a source of perpetual weakness and inefficiency.

These are, no doubt, difficulties, to a certain extent inherent in the institution; and, in order to overcome them, it is obvious that the discipline should have every help that can be given to it; that the powers granted to those who are to administer it should be fully as large and as little subject to cavil and controul as those which are found necessary in other places of education; that the system pursued should be marked by steadiness, uniformity, decision, promptness, and impartiality; and, particularly in reference to the two last difficulties, that there should be no doubt or delay in visiting with expulsion either such single acts as would be so punished at great schools and the Universities, or such a persevering violation of the rules of the college as either indicates an indisposition to the service, or a presumption that patronage or mistaken||lenity would, under any circumstances, prevent the entire loss of an appointment.

If it be asked, whether such have been the powers possessed, and such the system pursued, the answer must certainly be in the negative; and when it is known that very great adventitious difficulties in the government of the college have been added to the natural difficulties already noticed, it may not be a subject of surprise that those parts of the discipline most likely to be affected by such causes should have failed.

In the original constitution of the college, it was not thought expedient by its Founders to intrust the power of expulsion to the collegiate authorities. As expulsion involved the loss of a very valuable appointment, the Directors wished to reserve it in their own hands; and, in all cases of great importance, the Principal and Professors were directed to report to the Committee of College, and to wait their decision. It was in consequence believed by many students, that, unless the offence was peculiarly flagrant, they would run little risk of losing their appointments, and that their powerful friends in the India-house would make common cause with them in defeating the decisions of the College Council. This opinion seems to have commenced early, and to have diffused itself pretty generally; and there is little doubt that it contributed to facilitate the rise of that spirit of insubordination which began to manifest itself in the third year after the college was established. It must be obvious that no steady system of discipline could be maintained while the Principal and Professors were, on every important occasion, to appeal with uncertain effect to another body, where the student hoped that his personal interest would prevent any serious inconvenience. Yet this continued to be the constitution of the college for a period of six years, during which there were three considerable disturbances. On these occasions, of course, the Directors were called in; and although the more enlightened and disinterested portion of them, who saw the necessity of an improved education for their servants in India, were, unquestionably, disposed to do every thing that was proper to support the discipline; yet, the proceedings respecting the college were marked by an extraordinary want of energy, promptness, and decision, and indicated in the most striking manner the *disturbing* effects of private and contending interests. On occasion of the last of these disturbances in particular (that of 1812), the management of which the Court took entirely into their own hands, they detained a large body of students in town for above a month; and after entering into the most minute details, and subjecting all the parties to repeated examinations at the India-house,||came to no final decision. The case was then referred back again to the College Council, who were desired to select for expulsion a certain number of those concerned, who should appear to them to have been the most deeply engaged as ringleaders, and the least entitled to a mitigation of sentence on the score of character. When this was done, and a sentence of expulsion passed in consequence on five students, a subsequent Vote of the Court restored them *all* to the service, and they were sent out to India without even completing the usual period of residence at the college!!!

If we consider the real difficulties belonging to such an institution, in conjunction with the uncertain and inefficient system of government above described, and recollect, at the same time, that, from the very commencement of the college, there has been a large party connected with India entirely hostile to it, the gradual rise and prevalence of a spirit of insubordination in the college will appear to be vastly more natural and probable than a contrary spirit.

But when a spirit of insubordination and resistance
to discipline has once deeply infected any collected
body of persons, it is well known how strong a tendency it has to keep itself up; how easy, and almost
certainly, the contagion spreads to fresh comers; and
how extremely difficult it is effectually to eradicate it.

It is but a short time since the principal and professors of the East-India College have been legally
invested with those powers in the management of the
discipline which are found necessary at great schools
and the Universities, and which ought therefore unquestionably to have been given to them at the commencement of the institution. They are called upon to
correct and rectify a system of government which it
is at length acknowledged has been essentially defective for many years; and, strange to say, an inference
seems to be drawn against the whole establishment
because it is not already completed! Yet what is the
task they have to accomplish, and under what circumstances have they undertaken it? They have not
only to overcome by a steady and uniform system of
discipline, the natural difficulties inherent in the institution, but, by an union of conciliation, firmness, and
the strictest impartiality, to mitigate and gradually
extirpate the spirit of insubordination, which, by long
unskilful treatment, has infected the institution; and
this is to be done, not only without the cordial co-
operation of all the natural patrons and protectors of
the college, but with a spirit of direct hostility in a considerable body of the Directors and Proprietors, and
a disposition in the public to take part with those
from whom they hear most of the college, with little

or no inquiry into the real merits of the case. The practical effect of this hostility is nearly the same as if the authorities in the college did not yet possess full powers in the management of the discipline; and|| as no sentence of importance has yet been passed without occasioning a minute inquiry and investigation, which puts the college, as it were, regularly upon its defence, and very few, without giving rise to a most determined and persevering opposition, it is quite impossible that the students should be fully impressed with the idea that the power of punishing really rests in that quarter, where all parties would agree that it must be the most effectual in repressing acts of insubordination.

A further evil consequence of this hostility is, that language is publicly used, and reports generally circulated, calculated to fill the minds of the students with the most unfavorable prejudices. In general, when a parent sends his son to a school, or to the University, he endeavours to impress him with a respect for the place to which he is going, and the authorities to which he will be subject. It is to be feared that some young men come to the East-India College with very different impressions;—with the impression of having heard the college abused, and its downfal prognosticated, by those whom they must of course look up to as the persons that ought to influence their feelings and direct their conduct. It is scarcely possible that the students who come to the college thus prejudiced should ever feel that attachment to the place of their education, the effects of which are on every account so desirable; and it is difficult to conceive that an uniform spirit of order and obedience should prevail among those who have frequently heard that another *row* would destroy the college, and effect that object which they had been taught to consider as desirable. It is not meant to be asserted that any of the patrons or friends of the students have directly incited them to rebellion; but that the opinions which they have held, and the incautious language which they have used, must upon young minds necessarily have produced the same effects.

Whether it is possible for any set of men contending against such disadvantages, to make the college what it ought to be, is a point on which it is difficult to pronounce a decided opinion. At all events, it will be allowed that time is necessary as well as attention and ability.

Independently of other difficulties, time alone can overcome those that essentially and unavoidably belong to every new institution. If the proper executive powers had been given to the college at first, and it had been at all times fully supported by its founders and patrons, it would certainly have been rash to have pronounced finally on its competence or incompetence to fulfil its intended purpose, in a less time than that which has now elapsed since its foundation—about ten years. But these powers, though now formally granted, cannot yet appear to the students to be un-||disputed, and can scarcely have begun to have their natural operation. Surely, therefore, it would be still more rash to pronounce finally on what may be done, in a less time than another ten years; as it will be allowed that a considerable portion of that period must unavoidably be spent in correcting the effects of past errors.

The main and almost single object to be accomplished, is to eradicate the tendency to occasional acts of insubordination.

Notwithstanding the late virulent attacks, it may be confidently asserted that this tendency, and the unpleasant consequences which necessarily result from it, form the only just ground for stating that the college has not fairly answered the purpose for which it was instituted.

When the general good order of the college is considered, notwithstanding the natural difficulties adverted to in the beginning of this section, it is scarcely possible to conceive that this evil should not be susceptible of cure. But, to produce this effect, it is necessary that a full and perfect conviction of the stability of the institution, and the steadiness with which the collegiate authorities are able to maintain their decisions, should by repeated experience be fully impressed on the students.

That this has not yet been done, the persevering efforts that have been made to shake some late decisions, and the idea that has prevailed that an application would be made to Parliament to withdraw its legislative sanction from the establishment, afford sufficient proofs. And till this has been done, it may confidently be asserted, that nothing approaching to a fair experiment has been made of the practicability of removing the only essential evil of which the college justly stands chargeable.

The supply of competent and well-disposed servants

to fill the high official situations of India, is the object to be accomplished; and that plan which, consistently with the present legal and constitutional relations of the Company with the Government, most effectually attains this object, is the plan which ought to receive the sanction and support of the Legislature.

If the Legislature thinks that the institution of the college was an error, and that the acknowledged and glaring deficiency in the education of the Company's civil servants upon the old system, may be supplied in some other way more effective, and less subject to difficulties, let it at once be abolished. But if no plan presents itself which holds out a fair prospect of doing what is specifically wanted better than the one actually established, let the existing institution be supported in such a manner as to put an end to all that doubt and uncertainty which is so fruitful a source of offences. If the statutes and regulations of the college are faulty, there are legal means of altering them: if the Principal or||Professors are from any cause whatever incompetent to their situations, all or any of them may be removed: but if the establishment itself be a proper one, and destined to answer a very important purpose, it should be so fully and cordially supported as not to be liable to be shaken by the caprices of a few young men. Such caprices it is impossible to answer for in an establishment not as yet sufficiently sanctioned by time, and to which the parents and friends of many of the students are known to be hostile. But by steadiness within, and strong support without, they may undoubtedly be rendered at first ineffectual, and by degrees be prevented from shewing themselves in acts of insubordination.

It has been sometimes stated as extremely hard that a young man and his parents should suffer so severe a loss as that of an appointment to India on account of a few irregularities in early youth; but this argument, if it were allowed, would be conclusive against all laws. It is surely still harder that a man should sometimes suffer capitally for irregularly supplying some of the most pressing wants of nature.

But even with reference solely to places of education, the East-India College is by no means the only one where valuable property may be lost by misconduct in early youth. At Winchester, for instance, the boys on the foundation succeed in a regular course to fellowships at New College, Oxford, which may be considered almost in the light of a provision for life, and are valued by parents accordingly; yet on one occasion, not many years since, a greater number was expelled, and lost this valuable provision, than has been expelled during the course of the ten years that the East-India College has been established, although in the one case the institution was old, and in the other new. Many other instances might be mentioned of considerable loss of property incurred by misconduct in an early age at our great public seminaries.

It will however very rarely happen that a young man, whose habits and attainments would qualify him to become an useful servant of the Company, should be so unfortunate as to subject himself to the punishment of expulsion. Such a case, however, may possibly happen, and, when it does, it must be considered as a painful, but necessary, sacrifice to those general rules, the gross violation of which cannot be passed over without a sacrifice of much greater and more general interests than those of an individual and his connexions.

With regard to young men of a very different description, it cannot surely be a matter of regret, in any public view at least, that those who have shewn headstrong, refractory, and capricious tempers, united with habits of idleness and dissipation, should not be allowed to go out to India, and be furnished with an opportunity||of tyrannising over its suffering inhabitants, and of bringing the English name into hatred and disgrace. All the offices in India may not require talents; but all must require a certain degree of industry, good conduct, and inclination to service. And, beyond all question, one of the most important uses that the college can answer, one of the means by which it may confer the most extensive benefits upon India, is, by separating from the service those whose habits appear to be of a nature only to encumber, impede, and injure it.

The collegiate authorities now legally possess the power both of expelling, and of refusing certificates; but, unfortunately, from the disposition shown by the founders and patrons of the college, and that part of the public connected with India, in every case where the loss of an appointment is in question, a full support in the exercise of this power cannot be depended upon; although there can be no doubt that every act of collegiate punishment that is unopposed and unquestioned tends to render such acts in future less necessary; and every act that is so opposed and questioned tends to increase the probability of the recurrence of that conduct which had called it forth.

If this difficulty could be removed, the best hopes might be entertained of the result. And if the college were so supported, as to enable it gradually to subdue the spirit of insubordination, by removing refractory and vicious characters without clamour or cavil, and to exercise its discretionary powers in refusing certificates, according to the letter and spirit of its statutes, and with a view to the real interests of the service and the good of India, there is the strongest reason to presume, from the testimonies of what the college has already done, and the further good effects which might be confidently expected from the results just adverted to, that it would answer, in no common degree, the important purpose for which it was intended.

SECTION VII.—*Are the more general charges which have lately been brought against the college in the Court of Proprietors founded in truth? or are they capable of distinct refutation by an appeal to facts?*

It has been stated already in Section VI. that the only plausible grounds for saying that the college has not fully answered its purpose are the occasional disturbances which have taken place in it; and these disturbances have been traced to the difficulties which have been constantly thrown in the way of a firm and uniform exercise of collegiate authority. But in the Court of Proprietors, on the 18th of December, the most unmeasured accusations of every kind were heaped on the college. Mr. Hume is said to have||

affirmed, that, instead of its being a place where young men are formed in their morals, prepared in their character, and qualified in their education, it was the disgrace of England, and of every person connected with it; that it was incessantly the scene of riot, disorder, and irregularity; and that the inhabitants, who lived in the neighbourhood, were in a state of perpetual dread and alarm from the wanton excesses committed by the students.

These are indeed most serious charges; and if they were true, or even approaching to the truth, such a state of things must have produced a very marked deterioration of character in the young men who have gone out to India from the college. But, instead of this deterioration, what are the accounts from Calcutta? They are, that Lord Minto, Governor-General, the College Council of Fort William, Captain Roebuck, the Secretary of the College and Examiner, and Mr. Edmonstone, the first in Council, have all left written testimonies that a very great and general improvement had been conspicuous in the conduct of the students who had passed through the college at Hertford, and that they stood honourably distinguished, in the language of Lord Minto, "for regular attendance, for obedience to the statutes and discipline of the college, for orderly and decorous demeanour, for moderation in expense, and consequently in the amount of their debts, and, in a word, for those decencies of conduct which denote men well born, and characters well trained." Now, it is well known, that some little jealousy and fear of the college in England have occasionally prevailed among the friends of the college in Calcutta, owing to the idea, that the use of the latter might be superseded by the establishment of the former. Such testimonies are therefore the more honourable to those who gave them, and the more to be trusted by those who really wish to know the practical effects of the college in England on the conduct of the Company's junior servants in India. And under these circumstances they must be considered as *facts* which furnish a direct contradiction to the affirmation of Mr. Hume. They shew that, in the judgment of the most competent and disinterested authorities, the students at the East-India college *are formed in their morals, prepared in their character, and qualified in their education,* for the important stations they are likely to fill, and that the Hertford college, instead of being the disgrace of England, has been rendering, and is rendering, most essential service to India.

I certainly would have no connexion with an institution which could *justly* be considered as the disgrace of England; but I should think it a pusillanimous desertion of a good cause if I were to allow myself to be driven away by a clamour which I know to be found-||ed either in interest and prejudice, or in an utter ignorance of what the college really is.

The testimonies above alluded to,[2] and more fully detailed in Section V., are really of the kind to determine whether the college answers its purpose or not; but, instead of referring to any such *facts,* or

---

[2] These testimonies are further confirmed by the letters of all the most distinguished students in India who have passed through the college in England, and by all the civil servants I have met with who have returned from India within the last five or six years, without a single exception.

endeavouring to get information from competent and disinterested judges, who have spent some time in the college, and have been astonished at the scene of order and regularity which they witnessed, after the absurd rumours they had heard on the subject, Mr. Hume seems to have sought for the character of the college from fathers irritated at the merited punishment of their sons, and from some Hertfordshire country gentlemen, tremblingly alive about their game,—two of the most suspicious quarters from which information could possibly be obtained.

Every man acquainted with our Universities and public schools must know, that young persons may come to them from a domestic education, apparently innocent, and yet in less than two years richly deserve to be expelled. Instances of the kind have fallen within my own observation at Cambridge, and yet I mean to send my only son there, if I can afford it, as the best place of education that I know. But in the instance about which Mr. Hume seems to have made so silly a parade, I believe there was never any question of innocence. Let Mr. Hume candidly and manfully produce the name of the person who is now become an outcast of society from the contagion of the East-India college. Let his previous character be traced; and let it be seen, by *an appeal to facts,* whether he was not much more likely to corrupt others than to be corrupted himself. His example indeed could hardly have failed to produce a most pernicious effect, if the good sense and moral feelings of the great majority of the students had not induced them, from the very first term of his residence, to shun his society.

It is utterly astonishing to me that a man of sense, a man of the world, and a friend to the good government of India, as I before thought Mr. Hume was, should lend himself to retail the ebullitions of disappointed fathers, who, however justly they may be pitied, are the very last persons that should be heard as authorities, particularly as it is known that there have been persons of this description, who, after having vainly attempted by misrepresentations and menaces to intimidate the college authorities, have most impru-||dently and rashly, as well as wickedly, vowed to pursue them with the most determined hatred and hostility.

With regard to the country gentlemen of Hertfordshire, the other suspicious source from which Mr. Hume appears to have derived his information, they are of very high respectability, and I feel much indebted to them for the uniform personal kindness and attention they have shewn me; but I cannot conceal from myself, nor can they conceal from me, that, with one or two splendid exceptions,[3] they have been from the very first enemies of the college. They prophesied early that the building would become a barrack, and their conduct has not been unfavourable to the accomplishment of their prediction. It would seem to be from this quarter, or some of their friends, that the materials were furnished for the querulous paragraph in the *Times* about the Principal being made a justice

---

[3] The most distinguished one is Lord John Townshend, the nearest neighbour of the college, whose property almost surrounds it.

of the peace without a foot of land in the county.[4] Now I would willingly appeal to the most competent judges of the persons who ought or ought not to be made justices of the peace, with a view to the maintenance of the police of the country, whether the head of so large an establishment as that of the East-India college, situated two miles distant from any town, should not be one. The appointment was recommended by the President of the Board of Controul, Lord Buckinghamshire; and though it has never been used, and probably never will, in the maintenance of discipline, as it relates to students, it was unquestionably a highly proper one. Such observations, therefore, on this subject, as those in the *Times,* only throw ridicule on the persons who make them.

Having mentioned the *Times,* I cannot help noticing the novel and strange doctrines promulgated in a scurrilous paragraph about the college, on the 27th of December, in answer to *Maro,* who has no connexion with the college. I could not have conceived it possible that any English writer, with the slightest pretension to character, would have dared to avow that a lad of seventeen or eighteen, who offends against the criminal laws of his country, is not amenable to those laws, because he happens to be a gentleman's son, and to be resident at some school or college. The editor of the *Times* has made this sentiment his own by the manner in which he has inserted it; other-

[4] Dr. Batten, as a clergyman having a considerable benefice in Lincolnshire, is as legally qualified to become a justice of the peace as any magistrate on the bench, nor was his appointment in any respect different from any other justice of the peace in the county, as falsely asserted by the *Times.*

wise I should have thought that it could only||have come from the father of some worthless sons, who, being conscious that they were likely to commit offences deserving of imprisonment, pillory, and *public* whipping, was very desirous, as he might well be, of finding some plea for getting him off with a *private* flogging. With regard to the scandalous and libellous insinuation at the end of the paragraph in question, let every inquiry be made on the subject, and the more minute and accurate it is, the more agreeable it will be to the college.

But to return to the country gentlemen of Hertfordshire; I can most readily enter into their feelings, in not liking an establishment of eighty young men, from sixteen to twenty, in their immediate neighbourhood. Had I the choice of settling in a country residence, I should certainly avoid the vicinity of Oxford or Cambridge, Eton or Harrow. They may be fairly allowed, therefore, to wish for the removal of the college; but on that very account they may be legitimately challenged as witnesses against it, at least till they come forward with their names, and produce specific charges. Let some three or four of them, and the same number of the respectable inhabitants of Hertford, declare conscientiously, and on their honour, "that the inhabitants in the neighbourhood of the college live in a state of perpetual dread and alarm, from the wanton excesses committed by the students," and I will then believe what I have not the slightest ground for believing at present; but, till some such proof as this is offered, I maintain that an appeal to *facts* would shew that the asseveration of Mr. Hume is absolutely untrue, and founded on some grossly false, and probably anonymous information.

Of the general conduct of the students, I can affirm, from my own knowledge, that they are beyond all comparison more free from the general vices that relate to wine, women, gaming, extravagance, riding, shooting, driving, than the under graduates at our universities; and, I really believe, more free than the head classes of our great schools. If I were to send my son to the East-India college, I should feel he was in a safer situation in all these respects than either at Eton or Cambridge. To those who will not judge on these subjects by comparison, but, without any knowledge or experience of what can be done with young people, have formed Utopian views of youthful innocence and perfection, which they expect to see realised, I have nothing to say.

Mr. Randle Jackson has been pleased to state, that he does not mean to propose the abolition of the establishment, but merely its reformation, and conversion into a school. He thinks that the education given at the college is not of the right kind, and that it is not necessary to make young men mount to the higher rank in||literature, in order to teach them "to weigh tea, count bales, and measure muslins."

If the main business of the great majority of the civil servants of the Company really were to weigh tea, count bales, and measure muslins, something might, perhaps, be said for Mr. Jackson's opinion; but what is the statement of the ablest Governor-General that India ever saw? It is, "that commercial and mercantile knowledge is not only unnecessary throughout every branch of the judicial department (which includes much more than half of the service), but those civil servants who are invested with the powers of magistracy, or attached to the judicial department in any ministerial capacity, although bearing the denomination of merchants, factors, or writers, are bound by law, and by the solemn obligation of an oath, to abstain from every commercial and mercantile pursuit." * * * * * *"*No more arduous or complicated duties of magistracy exist in the world, no qualifications more various and comprehensive can be imagined, than those which are required from every British subject who enters the seat of judgment within the limits of the Company's empire in India.*" These are the offices for which Mr. Randle Jackson, in a fine vein of irony and eloquence, laughs at the absurdity of sending out well-educated men, under the happy image of a little army of Grotiuses and Puffendorfs.

But the judicial, though the largest, is far from being the sole department quite unconnected with trade. The financial and political departments employ a considerable body of the civil servants; and the *fact* really is, that, out of four hundred and forty-two persons in the civil service in Bengal, only seventy-two, including the collectors of the customs, have any connexion with trade; and even these, Lord Wellesley says, should have many of the qualifications of statesmen.[5] Such being the *facts,* according to the testimonies of the Marquis Wellesley, and the Indian Register, which, I presume, are better authorities than

---

[5] See Sect. I. p. 476.

that of Mr. Jackson, is it not perfectly obvious that the education of the civil servants should be fitted for the high and important stations held by the great body of them, and that those who are comparatively unsuccessful in the career of improvement should supply the departments where less abilities are required? To talk then, in the present state of India, of an education fitted for weighing tea, counting bales, and measuring muslins, betrays a degree of ignorance and folly, of which I did not think Mr. Randle Jackson capable.||

But Mr. Jackson is not satisfied with saying that the education at the East-India college does not accord with his own narrow views on the subject. He joins lustily in the clamour about violence and licentiousness, and then, with a view to give greater force to his next argument, he observes, that it would be a great palliative of this general misconduct if the friends of the college could come forward, and refer to their progress in literature, as a counterpoise to their boyish levities; but that unfortunately this could not be done, as would appear by an extract he would read from a Report furnished by the college itself. Now, notwithstanding this extract and others, the false inferences from which I will presently advert to, I, as *a friend* of the college, and with much better opportunities of information on the subject than Mr. Jackson, do come forward and assert that its literature has been on the whole eminently successful; that the papers produced at every public examination shew no common degree of industry and talent in the various branches of learning to which they are applied;

and that the progress made in the Oriental languages is clearly and irrefragably proved by the rapidity with which the students from the East-India college are able to qualify themselves for the final examination at the college of Fort William; and, consequently, that an appeal to *facts* directly contradicts Mr. Jackson's assertion. Let the Oriental Visitor, Dr. Wilkins, be asked his opinion on the subject; and, though I well know he differs from me on some points relating to the form of the institution, I know he is too honourable a man not to avow in public what he has distinctly said to me in private; namely, that the very short time in which a large portion of the students now pass through the college at Calcutta is a clear proof that they must have come from a good place of education for the Oriental languages at home.

With regard to the extract first read by Mr. Jackson, it seems to have been taken from the Report of the Oriental Visitor in December, 1815, in which it appeared that a certain number of students, (five, I believe, out of twenty-nine) had been unable to pass the Oriental test. To draw from this circumstance an inference that the Oriental languages had not been well taught at the East-India college would be the same as to infer that education at Cambridge was extremely ill conducted, because some men almost every year are refused their degrees; or that the classics were not well taught at Eton or Westminster, because they send forth every year into the world some incorrigible blockheads. The proper inference, in general, ought only to have been, that the students in question were not proper persons to send out to

India.||But, in the individual instance referred to, there really was something to be said for them. It was the very first time that the Oriental test had been applied; it was in some respects an *ex post facto* law, not having been announced till the third term of the residence of those students who were first subjected to it; and they were, further, not sufficiently aware of the nature and extent of it. Whether this was a sufficient excuse for the petition made to the Court, and the indulgence granted, I will not venture to give an opinion, thinking it quite immaterial to the question. In the next examination of May, 1816, only one failed, and was detained another term; and, in the one just passed, none failed. This last examination indeed has been particularly distinguished by extraordinary eminence in some departments of Oriental literature, combined with the most successful exertions in European studies.

The next document adverted to by Mr. Jackson, from which he seems absurdly to have drawn very large inferences, is a confidential Report, of May, 1816, made by the College Council to the Committee of College in the India-house, candidly describing those fluctuations in the amount and direction of the mass of talent and industry in the college, which must necessarily take place in every institution in which the studies are various. It is a homely, but a true, saying, that you may bring a horse to the water, but cannot make him drink; and, though all the students at the East-India college are required to attend the stated lectures appointed for them, on pain of impositions, yet no rational person can suppose that their attention can be directed, at all times, in the same measure and quantity, to each. Could any thing on earth be more natural than that, when a test was appointed in the Oriental languages *exclusively,* the students should think that Oriental literature was more highly appreciated by the Honourable Court of Directors than the other branches of learning taught at the college, and that they ought, therefore, to direct towards it a greater portion of their time? And yet the relation of this simple fact has been twisted into an inference that the students at the East-India college are allowed to do just as they like with regard to the choice of their studies. What a prodigious ardour for misrepresentation does this shew! I will just add, in reference to the last paragraph of the extract on which so much stress has been laid, that if such a report was unhappily required from the great schools of the country, and was given with the same frankness, it would appear that no very inconsiderable proportion of the boys might fairly be said, *in spite of the rod,* to have abandoned the only studies of the place.

The extraordinary part of this business is, not the Report||itself, but the place where it is now to be found,—the public newspapers!!! It may shortly be expected that the monthly Reports of conduct, which have lately been required, will be published in the same way, and that the gentlemen of the college will be subjected to prosecutions for libellous aspersions on the characters of some of the students, by calling them irregular. In point of fact, the formal threat of a prosecution for a libel, through the channel of a lawyer's letter, was really sent to the Registrar of the College not long since, in consequence of a detailed Report being required of the character of a young man, whose certificate it was impossible for the College Council, consistently with their duty, to grant.

But to return to Mr. Randle Jackson. The great weight and force of his eloquence seem to have been directed to show the use and advantage of flogging, and the disadvantage of caps and gowns. He is reported to have pronounced, with very great energy, the following pithy maxim: "That those who did not *learn* should be made to *feel;*" and the sentiment seems to have been received by repeated and long-continued cheers.

Now flogging may be a very good thing in itself, but I am totally at a loss to conceive what Mr. Randle Jackson, and his friends in the *Times,* can mean by considering it as a *substitute* for expulsion. Let any master of a great school in the kingdom be asked whether he could maintain discipline by mere flogging, unsupported by the power of sending his boys away; and, unless his opinion is given in direct contradiction to his practice, he will say, that it is perfectly impossible. Only the other day, four or five boys were expelled from Harrow. Last year, five, I believe, or more, were expelled from Eton. And experience shows that even the black-hole and military discipline will not do.[6] At this present moment *five* are banished from

---

[6] No Englishman will, I trust, venture to propose a military system for the education of the future administrators of justice in India. This would be taking hints from the late Emperor of France with a vengeance. But, after all, it appears, that it will not supersede banishment and dismission.

the military seminary of the Honourable the East-India Company, at Addiscombe, of the merits and efficacy of which so much has been said.

One would really think that the people who talk about the wonderful effects of corporal correction had not only never been at a great school themselves, but had never seen a man who had been at one. A more chimerical project scarcely ever entered into the|| brain of a visionary than that of superseding the use of expulsion among youths of sixteen by mere school-flogging.[7]

With regard to caps and gowns they are evidently useful in discipline, by rendering concealment more difficult; and pointing out the individuals, who may be occasionally seen without them, as bound upon some expedition contrary to the regulations of the college. And if, in addition to this obvious use, they have, in the present case, contributed to inspire some manly feelings rather earlier than usual, they have, in my view of the subject, been of service. The objections, which have been made by Mr. Jackson and others to this innocent badge, are perfectly ridiculous. As to the Universities, they must be much above feel-

---

[7] Not long after Dr. Keate became head master of Eton, he is said to have flogged eighty boys in one day, most of them above sixteen. But what gave him the power of exercising this act of discipline? Solely and exclusively the power of saying, "If you do not submit, you no longer belong to Eton school." Nor would the *threat* have been sufficient, if it had not been known that he could have put it in execution without the slightest opposition, and would unquestionably have done so if the boys had not complied. With such a power of expulsion, heavy impositions are probably as effective as flogging; but without such a power, neither the one nor the other can maintain discipline.

ing the slightest jealousy on the subject; and every rational man belonging to them must heartily laugh at the laudable zeal of the London citizens, to inspire them with a becoming dread of such a horrible usurpation.

If the Honourable Court of Directors, sanctioned by the Legislature, should determine to abolish the establishment in Hertfordshire as a college, I do most earnestly and most conscientiously recommend to them not to have any *appropriate* institution for the education of their civil servants. They may entirely rely upon it that the main difficulty attending the present establishment, instead of being removed, will, in some respects, be aggravated by its conversion into a school, and they will entirely fail in accomplishing what ought to be the great objects of an education for the Indian civil service. If I were to describe a narrow education, one the least calculated to infuse a "spirit of British justice into the government of sixty millions of Asiatics," it would be the taking boys at thirteen from the common schools of the country, placing them in a seminary where the Oriental languages were considered as the only passport to India till sixteen, and then sending them into offices up the country to act as copying-clerks, with only one or two, perhaps narrow-minded Euro-||peans to converse with,—a system expressly and specifically reprobated by Lord Wellesley. When a youth is reading Demosthenes and Cicero, or even Homer and Virgil, he is unquestionably gaining something besides mere words, something that will tend to invigorate, enlarge, and improve his mind; but, when he is applying to the

Oriental languages, he is really getting little more than the possession of an instrument. Of the great importance, and indeed absolute necessity, of this instrument for the service in India, it is impossible for any man to be more convinced than myself. I believe even that I was the first that proposed the present test in the Oriental languages, as the absolute condition of a final appointment to India. It is unquestionably true that no important station in the East can or ought to be held by persons not acquainted with these languages. It is equally true that no important situation under the French government ought to be held by a person who does not understand French. But it really appears to me that it is taking as narrow a view of the subject to consider the Oriental languages as *all*, or nearly all, that is necessary in the education for the civil service, as to say that any man who understands French is qualified to be a French judge or a French minister of state.

Far better than such a narrow education, still embarrassed with all the difficulties about expulsion, would be the taking boys from the common schools of the country at about seventeen, and subjecting them to a strict examination in classical literature, and in the rudiments of the Oriental languages: the first to show that they had received the education of gentlemen, and that their minds were improved and capable of improvement; and the second to ascertain that they had made some progress in the languages absolutely necessary to their future destination. These are specific qualifications which might be distinctly described, and it might be left to the parents of those who were likely to be appointed, to put their sons in a way to acquire them wherever they might choose.

This system would, without doubt, be better calculated to give able servants to the Company, than the narrow education just described. But still it would be subject to great disadvantages; and, independently of the loss of the more general education which is given in the present college, and seems to have had the best effect in invigorating and improving the mind, there would be nothing to break the sudden transition from school discipline to the perfect liberty of a residence in India.

If I had no connexion with the college, or with India, further than the interest which every Englishman ought to feel in the good||government of the Indian territories, and yet could speak with the same knowledge of the subject as I can now, after an attention to it for ten years, I am confident that I should say that the specific object which ought to be aimed at by the Honorable Company, in the education for the civil service, is precisely that which is so much reprobated by Mr. Jackson, and others in various quarters, namely, that of endeavouring to inculcate, gradually, manly feelings, manly studies, and manly self-controul, rather earlier than usual. Those who go out to India, must and will be men the moment they reach the country, at whatever age that may be; and there they will be immediately exposed to temptations of no common magnitude and danger. To prepare them for this ordeal, Mr. Jackson and the silly writers in the *Times* recommend their being whipped till the last hour of their getting into their ships. I own it appears to me that the object is more likely to be attained by a gradual initiation into a greater degree of liberty, and a greater habit of depending upon themselves, than is usual at schools, carried on for two or three years previously, in some safer place than Calcutta.

The attempt is not without its difficulties, and may be subject to partial failure; but I am quite convinced that it is mainly to the success of this attempt, notwithstanding the tremendous obstacles which have been opposed to it, that the great and general improvement in the conduct of the students at Calcutta must be attributed; and if the college is destroyed, and boys are sent out to India fresh from the rod, it will soon be seen that this improved conduct will no longer be remarkable.

The *system* of the college is, I really believe, not far from what it ought to be.[8] That there are faults in the administration of it will be readily allowed, some perhaps within, (for what administration is faultless?) but many more and much greater without. Among these are the multiplicity of its governors,

---

[8] Little other change is wanting than that an appointment should be considered, in spirit and in truth, not in mere words, as a prize to be contended for, not a property already possessed, which may be lost. If the Directors were to appoint one-fifth every year, beyond the number finally to go out, and the four-fifths were to be the best of the whole body, the appointments would then really be prizes to be contended for, and the effects would be admirable. Each appointment to the college would then be of less value, but they would be more in number, and the patronage would hardly suffer. A Director could not then indeed be able to send out an unqualified son. But, is it fitting that he should? This is a fair question for the consideration of the Legislature and the British Public.

consisting not only of the Court of Directors, but of the Court of Proprietors;—the variety of opinions among them, some being for a college in England, some for a college in Calcutta, some for a school, and|| some for nothing at all;—the constant discussion arising from this variety of opinion, which keeps up a constant expectation of change;—the interest of individuals to send out their sons as early, and with as little expense of education, as possible, an interest too strong for public spirit;—the very minute and circumstantial details, in all the proceedings of the college which are required to be seen by all the ladies and gentlemen who are proprietors of India stock;—the impossibility of sending a student away without creating a clamour from one end of London to the other, greatly aggravated and lengthened by the power thus furnished, of debating every step of the proceedings;—the chances that the details above adverted to will enable some ingenious lawyer to find a flaw in the proceedings, with a view to their reversal;—the never-ending applications made to the college, when a student is sent away, for readmission, assuming every conceivable form of flattery and menace;—the opinion necessarily formed, and kept up in this way among the students, that sentences, though passed, will not be final;—and, above all, the knowledge they must have, from the avowed wish of many of the proprietors of East-India stock to destroy the college, that a rebellion would be agreeable to them.

How is it possible to answer for the conduct of young men, under such powerful excitements from without? For my own part, I am only astonished that the college has been able to get on at all, under these overwhelming obstacles; and that it has got on, and done great good too, (which I boldly assert it has,) is no common proof of its internal vigour, and its capacity to answer its object.

The present virulent attack upon the college has been meditated some time; and it could hardly fail to be known to the students that a disturbance this autumn would have been hailed by many of the Court of Proprietors as the happiest omen of success. Under these circumstances, the orderly conduct of the students for the last year does them the highest honor. And it is not a little discreditable to the character of the present attack, and the motives which have dictated it, that it was brought forward, not at a time when an unhappy act of violence might have given some plausible ground for it, but after a period of great quiet and order, and at the conclusion of a term eminently distinguished for great industry, and successful literary exertion.||